The
ASTRAL
PROJECTION
WORKBOOK

In the same series

THE ASTROLOGY WORKBOOK
  Cordelia Mansall
THE CHINESE ASTROLOGY WORKBOOK
  Derek Walters
THE CRYSTAL WORKBOOK
  Ursula Markham
THE DOWSER'S WORKBOOK
  Tom Graves
THE DREAMER'S WORKBOOK
  Nerys Dee
THE ESP WORKBOOK
  Rodney Davies
THE FORTUNE-TELLER'S WORKBOOK
  Sasha Fenton
THE GRAPHOLOGY WORKBOOK
  Margaret Gullan-Whur
THE MEDITATOR'S MANUAL
  Simon Court
THE NUMEROLOGY WORKBOOK
  Julia Line
THE PALMISTRY WORKBOOK
  Nathaniel Altman
THE PLAYING CARD WORKBOOK
  Joanne Leslie
THE PSYCHIC ENERGY WORKBOOK
  R.Michael Miller & Josephine M. Harper
THE REINCARNATION WORKBOOK
  J.H.Brennan
THE RUNIC WORKBOOK
  Tony Willis
THE TAROT WORKBOOK
  Emily Peach

The ASTRAL PROJECTION WORKBOOK

How To Achieve Out-of-Body Experiences

J. H. Brennan

 Sterling Publishing Co., Inc.   New York

Published in 1990 by
Sterling Publishing Co., Inc.
387 Park Avenue South
New York, New York 10016

ISBN 0-8069-7306-4

First published in the U.K. in 1989 by The Aquarian Press
This edition published by arrangement with the
Thorsons Publishing Group, Wellingborough, England
This edition available in the United States, Canada
and the Philippine Islands only.

Printed in the U.S.A.

Library of Congress Cataloging-in-Publication Data
Brennan, J. H.
    The astral projection workbook : how to achieve out-of-body
experiences / J. H. Brennan.
        p.   cm.
    ISBN 0-8069-7306-4
    1. Astral projection.   2. Astral projection—Problems, exercises,
etc.   I. Title.
BF1389.A7B74   1989
133.9—dc20   89-29668
                                                             CIP

1   3   5   7   9   10   8   6   4   2

Contents

Introduction

'Astral Projection' is one of those terms which, though widely used in esoteric circles, actually means different things to different people. To some it suggests stepping out of your physical body to make your way in the world like a ghost, passing through walls and doors while you are (generally) invisible to those still locked into solid flesh. To others, it is the projection of consciousness into another world altogether, the fabled Astral Plane, where the normal laws of physics no longer apply and all sorts of interesting weirdness may be experienced.

Although carrying the same label and far too often confused in occult literature, these two experiences are quite distinct. I have managed both – the latter far more often than the former – and they seem to me actually to involve different *mechanisms*. Certainly the techniques used to stimulate them are quite different.

In this workbook, I will deal with *both* forms of astral projection. But to avoid the old confusion, I propose to call the former (where you wander the familiar world like a ghost) *etheric projection* or *projection of the phantom*. The latter experience (where you enter a totally different world) I will call Astral Plane projection.

You should be aware that skill in one form of projection is no guarantee of expertise in the other. There are etheric projectors to whom the Astral Plane is as mysterious and alien as the far side of the moon. And there are Astral Plane projectors utterly unable to separate the phantom in the physical world. One benefit of this is that you need only practise the type of projection that interests you – there is no pressure on you to do both.

The first section of the *Astral Projection Workbook* deals with the projection of the phantom. It will introduce you to the concept of subtle bodies, show you how these bodies separate on death (and partly separate during sleep) then teach you how they may be consciously separated by almost anyone without going to the trouble of dying first.

The second section deals with Astral Plane projection. It discusses the Astral Plane itself, its nature and location, then shows how you may enter it by means of various techniques, including the specially constructed *astral doorways* which were the subject of the very first book I ever published.

Finally, having tried to clear up some of the confusion that exists concerning the two types of projection, I feel obliged to add to it by mentioning that an etheric projection can sometimes inadvertently cause you to slip onto the Astral Plane. By the time you have finished this workbook, you will hopefully know why.

Part One
ETHERIC PROJECTION

1.

The Living Ghosts

In 1845, a Livonian language expert named Mademoiselle Emilie Sagée was sacked from yet another teaching post. No one questioned her abilities, qualifications or skill; it was just that she upset her students . . . who could often see two of her. The second Mlle Sagée might be standing near the first beside the blackboard, or eating the same school dinner. Sometimes the second figure would sit quietly in a corner, watching the first at work. Sometimes it would leave her to get on with the lesson while it strolled through the school grounds. This was all too much for the directors of the School for Young Ladies near Riga. In the face of parental complaints, they suggested Mlle Sagée should pack her bags . . . as 18 other School Boards had already done before them.

Mlle Sagée might have had better luck teaching in Africa, where the Azande Tribe believe that everyone has two souls, one of which – the *mbisimo* – leaves the body during sleep. Or in Burma, where the second soul is likened to a butterfly. Or among the Bacairis of South America, who talk (like the Azande) of a *shadow* which travels out of the body when we fall asleep. In fact, when you get right down to research, it is quite surprising to find Mlle Sagée's talent caused any consternation at all. A survey has shown that no fewer than 57 cultures hold a firm belief in some sort of second body – and the list does not pretend to be definitive.

One of my earliest published short stories was called *House Haunting* and described how a young couple discovered the home of their dreams only to find it was on the market at a suspiciously low price. When they quizzed the estate agent, he reluctantly admitted the reason was because the house was haunted, but added, 'Don't worry, Madam – you're the ghost.'

The story drew on a factual case; and one that is particularly instructive. The woman (on whom the fictional wife was based) had been obsessed about her dream house for many years, creating and recreating it in her mind, imagining herself walking through its corridors and rooms. When, with her husband and the hapless estate agent, she discovered the house actually existed, she was able to describe the interior to the estate agent *before entering*. Her description was accurate in every detail except one: she spoke about a green door which did not actually exist. The agent was, however, able to confirm that such a door *had* existed, but had been bricked up a few years earlier.

As a novice author, I withheld several of the more bizarre details from my fictional account. I was convinced they would destroy the credibility of the story. In those days I was not aware how widespread this sort of phenomenon actually was.

Back in 1886, three founding fathers of the Society for Psychical Research, Gurney, Myers and Podmore, published a comprehensive tome entitled *Phantasms of the Living* which detailed 350 cases. In 1951, Sylvan Muldoon and Hereward Carrington added another 100 in their *Phenomena of Astral Projection*. Three years later, Hornell Hart was examining 288 cases in the *Journal of the American Society for Psychical Research*. Another psychical researcher, Robert Crockall, entered the lists in 1961 and between then and 1978 published no fewer than nine books of case histories. The scientist Celia Green appealed for information on the subject in the late 1960s, and had 360 replies from people with personal experience. John Poynton added 122 more in 1978. And doubtless by the time this book is published, even more material will have become available.

Typical of the sort of case investigated is an incident which occurred in 1863 when an American manufacturer named Wilmot was on board the *City of Limerick* when the ship hit a mid-Atlantic storm. During the night, he dreamed his wife visited him in her nightdress and kissed him. Although he had said nothing of the dream, his cabin-mate teased him the following morning about his midnight visit from a lady. When he arrived home in Bridgeport, Connecticut, his wife at once asked him if he had received a visit from her in the night. She had, she said, been worried by reports of shipwrecks and decided to try to find out if he was safe. Consequently she visualized herself flying over the ocean, finding the ship and going to his cabin. A man in the upper berth looked straight at her, but she went ahead and kissed her husband anyway. (Steve Richards makes the intriguing suggestion, in his *Traveller's Guide to the Astral Plane*, that she had planned to do more than kiss him, but was restrained by the presence of an audience.) When pressed, she was able accurately to describe the ship, the cabin and the man who had shared it with Mr Wilmot.

Although this is the sort of evidential case-study which finds its way into the textbooks, it is very clear that a great many people have out-of-body experiences of a less spectacular type – the sort of thing they might find personally impressive, but which would have nothing in it to convince an outsider.

Several years ago, for example, I was in bed preparing for sleep when I found myself standing at a crossroads about half a mile from my home. I glanced around in some confusion, then returned to my body with a substantial jerk. I am quite satisfied the experience was neither a dream nor a hallucination, but it is, of course, quite useless as evidence.

In this instance, minor as it was, I had at least the advantage of some theoretical knowledge of etheric projection. Others are not always so lucky. On one occasion I was visited by an 18-year-old woman rather desperately seeking advice on the treatment of epilepsy. Her 'symptoms' were those of spontaneous etheric projection. The epilepsy diagnosis had been delivered by a doctor when she was eight years old and she had been receiving regular drug therapy ever since.

What is happening here? Why should a woman's brooding cause an image of herself to appear in the cabin of a ship at sea, or in the house she was thinking about? How could Mlle Sagee appear in two places at once? What *is* the mbisimo of the Azande, the butterfly of Burma, the andadura shadow of the South American Bacairi? And is the whole thing some sort of pathology, the manifestation of epileptic brain patterns as my visitor's doctor believed? For answers, we have to venture into the daunting realms of occult anatomy.

Whatever the cultural statistics quoted earlier, Western thought, by and large, assumes you have only one body – the one that is holding this book at this moment. Even religious doctrines of *soul* and *spirit* tend to conjure up formless abstractions far more readily than concrete pictures.

In Ancient Egypt, however, it was a common conceit that humanity had three souls. These were known as the *ba*, the *ka* and the *ib*. The ba was the bird-soul, the ib was the heart, but the ka, interestingly, was known as the *double*. Egyptians believed it to be a mirror image of the physical body, but composed of finer matter. The ka, under a variety of different names, would be recognized instantly by yoga initiates of India, Tibet and China. Many yoga systems actually postulate a whole series of subtle bodies, one within the other, like a set of Russian dolls. This notion, carried into Europe and America by Madame Blavatsky and her Theosophists, has taken firm root in Western esoteric thought.

How many bodies you actually have depends to some extent on the particular sub-system you are studying, but most authorities include an *etheric* (sometimes called *astral* or *desire body*), a *mental* and a *spiritual*. Each has its own characteristics, function and sphere of operation. Each is composed of progressively finer material.

In this section, the only body we will be dealing with is the *etheric*, although we will be returning briefly to the others when we reach Section Two of the workbook dealing with the Astral Plane.

While it is true to say that science in general does not recognize the etheric body, some scientists certainly do – and a few of the more open-minded (or perhaps merely eccentric) have tried to find out more about it.

In the 1920s, for example, a macabre series of experiments was carried out by Dr Duncan McDougall of Haverhill, Mass., who decided to *weigh* those of his patients who were in the process of dying from tuberculosis. To do so, he placed them – bed and all – on a delicately balanced scale . . . and waited. As death occurred, he discovered, in four out of six cases, a weight loss varying between two and two-and-a-half ounces. The conclusion drawn was that *something* vacated the body on death and that while obviously invisible and intangible, it was at least sufficiently solid to have measurable weight.

Dr McDougall's approach had an elegant simplicity, but I am not aware of many scientists who have attempted to duplicate his experiments – possibly due to the difficulty of finding a reliable supply of terminal patients. There was, however, one couple who came to somewhat similar conclusions, albeit by a different route – the Dutch physicists Drs Malta and Zaalberg Van Zelst.

Working out of the Hague, the Van Zelsts invented – again in the 1920s – a very curious instrument called a *dynamistograph*. This apparatus, which had a pointer on a lettered dial at the top, was, so its inventors claimed, able to make direct contact with the spirit world. Left in a room by itself (and observed through a small window) the machine would be manipulated by spirits who spelled out lengthy messages. I am not entirely clear how the Drs Van Zelst used this device to measure the etheric body, but they subsequently claimed to have discovered it was capable of expanding by about 1/40,000,000 of its own volume and contracting by some 1/6,250,000. It was composed of 'extremely small and widely separated' atoms, had a density 176.5 times lighter than air and weighed, on average, 69.5 gr, or two-and-a-quarter ounces.

The dynamistograph sounds so like one of those 'futuristic' radio sets featured in the old *Flash Gordon* movies that it is difficult to take it seriously. And while Dr McDougall's work was interesting, perhaps even important, his methodology was distinctly bizarre. Only a decade or so later, however, another American scientist, Dr Harold Saxton Burr, anatomy professor at Yale, embarked on a series of experiments altogether more convincing.

Burr was interested in the electrical potential of living things, an area of research even more unpopular in the 1930s than it is today. He set up measuring equipment which would be considered crude now, but was nonetheless able to detect electrical field phenomena associated with trees and other plants, many animals, including humanity, and even slime moulds. Such fields are not static. A voltmeter attached to a tree will, for example, indicate fluctuations in response to light, moisture, storms, sunspots and moon phases. Over a period of years, Burr came to believe in the existence of a *life-field* which, in the words of Dr Lyall Watson, 'holds the shape of an organism just as a mould determines the shape of a pie or pudding.'

In his *Blueprint for Immortality*, Burr remarks, 'When we meet a friend we have not seen for six months, there is not one molecule in his face which was there when we last saw him. But thanks to his controlling life-field, the new molecules have fallen into the old, familiar pattern and we can recognize his face.' Dr Burr's theories were largely ignored by the scientific establishment throughout much of his working life, even though they went a long way towards explaining one of the most persistent mysteries of cellular biology. Simply stated, the mystery is how certain cells in your body 'knew' how to grow into a kidney, while others grew into a brain. Pancreatic tissue grafted onto your nose will never result in the growth of a new pancreas on your face. Sponges sieved through silk to separate their constituent cells will nevertheless reform as they were before. More impressive still, the cells of *two different* sponges may be sieved and mixed together without disrupting the process – they will re-form as separate individuals.

It has long been evident that some sort of organizing principle is involved in living matter and scientists have devoted substantial time and effort in a vain attempt to isolate chemical or other triggers of the process. In the absence of anything better, Dr Burr's life-field certainly seems to fit the bill. And if it has so far been greeted with little scientific enthusiasm, there is still some empirical evidence for a 'mould which holds the shape of the organism.'

Certain lizards are capable of shedding and regrowing their tails. Others – notably the little salamander – can regrow whole limbs. (In one unpleasant experiment, a young salamander was persuaded to replace all of its legs six times in a three-month period.) In 1958, an orthopaedic surgeon named Robert Becker tried to find out why a salamander could do this when a frog, a similar sort of amphibian, could not. Careful measurements enabled him to determine that the ends of both animals' limbs were charged with a negative current of 0.000002 amps – an almost undetectable flow. Becker then went on to amputate the right forelimb of both frog and salamander. When the operation was complete, he discovered there was still a tiny electrical flow in the stump, but the polarity had reversed.

As the frog's wounds healed, forming scar tissue, the positive polarity gradually reverted to the original negative flow. The salamander showed an entirely different pattern. The electrical potential of the limb first dropped, then rose to three times its normal level, turning negative in the process. This high negative charge was maintained until a whole new limb was regenerated, inside a few weeks.

As a surgeon, Becker was less concerned with pure research than practical application – he had embarked on his experiments in the hope of finding out why fractured bones sometimes refused to knit. Consequently he developed a tiny battery which produced a current mimicking that of the salamander. When implanted in the stump of a frog amputee, it regenerated the entire limb exactly as the salamander had done. In 1972, the first mammal (a laboratory rat) succeeded in the partial regeneration of a limb using a similar device. Since then, Becker has shown that the right sort of applied current can actually close holes in the heart, regenerate nerve tissue and inhibit infection. Thousands of patients world-wide have had the benefit of battery implants to aid bone healing in difficult fractures. Thousands more, including my wife, have used electrical stimulation to inhibit chronic pain.

While orthodox science still seems reluctant to discuss the theory, practical experience has very clearly established an electrical aspect to the human body. Technology has advanced so far since the time that Dr Burr first tried to measure a life-field that an investment of less than £100 will buy you equipment sufficiently sensitive to detect fluctuations in the electrical potential of the skin. I have one such device which is no larger than a ball point pen.

Occultists have a special interest in the work of Burr and Becker, for the notion of a life-field which holds the shape of an organism runs very close to some very old ideas about a second body. The use of the word *double* to describe the phantom is deceptive, for it suggests something patterned on the physical body. But many occultists – and particularly Qabalists – have long believed just the opposite. They have thought of the phantom as the *foundation* of the physical, the pre-existent pattern into which it grows. Esoteric doctrine is quite clear on this point, for it holds that in the case of an amputation, for example, the etheric body remains whole, which is the reason why some amputees feel pain or itching in their missing limbs.

There seems to me very little difference between Burr's life-field and the occult notion of an etheric body, except, perhaps, in one important respect. Dr Burr suggests the field is an integral part of a living creature, a phenomenon of living matter, possibly even the factor which, ultimately, differentiates between that which is animate and that which is not. Occultists,* however, believe that the life-field may – in the case of human beings at least – be temporarily separated from the physical body without causing harm to either. And in the process, the life-field may become the vehicle of consciousness and perception.

*Or some occultists. Dr Douglas Baker believes the etheric body can never separate from the physical body during life and considers an even more subtle body, the true astral, is involved in what I call etheric projection.

2.

What Happens When You Leave Your Body

Although members of the Hermetic Order of the Golden Dawn (an institution founded in 1887) were taught a method of etheric projection, they were sworn to secrecy about the technique. Consequently, as late as the middle 1920s, the psychic researcher Dr Hereward Carrington was unable to find any information at all on the subject beyond some experimental work carried out in France. The French experimenter was a M. Charles Lancelin who was interested in the effects of 'animal magnetism' a sadly confused subject now largely dismissed not only by science, but by occultists as well.

The history of animal magnetism dates back to the famous Franz Anton Mesmer, who believed a subtle fluid emerged both from metallic magnets and the human body; and could be used to cure a variety of illnesses. He developed a technique of 'magnetizing' patients so that they fell into a convulsive trance, from which they often emerged free of former ailments. As a healer, Mesmer was conspicuously successful and for some time very fashionable. But when the French Academy of Sciences was moved to investigate his claims, the committee discovered nothing that 'could not be explained by imagination.'

But what really put paid to animal magnetism was not the frantic efforts of the Establishment, but the entirely sympathetic work of a Mesmer admirer who was trying to follow his example.

The Marquis de Puysegur tried to magnetize a shepherd boy and found the lad fell into the type of passive trance we now call hypnotic. This development so confounded the historians of science that it is still quite common to find Mesmer referred to as the father of hypnosis, even though his techniques produced a totally different kind of trance.

M. Lancelin, it seems, was not confused and 'magnetized' subjects exactly as Mesmer had done. In their magnetized state, he was able to extract, so to speak, the etheric body from the physical body and set up a number of ingenious tests to show when this had been achieved. He believed a certain type of temperament was necessary for success but his discussion of sanguine, lymphatic, nervous, and bilious subjects seems outmoded, even quaint, today . . . as, of course, does the use of 'magnetism' itself.

Dr Carrington summarized Lancelin's work in a book called *Modern Psychical Phenomena* and later expanded on the subject in his *Higher Psychical Develop-*

ment. He admitted he found the material in both books 'most inadequate', but it represented everything he could unearth at the time. Better days were, however, just around the corner.

In November 1927, Dr Carrington received a letter from an individual named Sylvan Muldoon, who claimed to have forgotten more about etheric projection than Lancelin ever knew. He enlarged on a number of points Lancelin had made and took issue with him on several others. Everything he said was, he claimed, drawn from personal experience. Muldoon was 25 years old in 1927. He had had his first out-of-body projection at the age of 12.

Carrington was impressed. He visited Muldoon and, despite finding him so seriously ill that his condition was considered terminal, conducted experiments to test his claims, then encouraged him to write a book on his experiences. Muldoon did, from his sickbed; and *The Projection of the Astral Body* (which credits Carrington as co-author) became a classic which is now in its fifth reprint, and helping train a third generation of projectors. Despite the use of the term *astral* in the title, Dr Carrington makes clear in his introduction to the book that Muldoon is dealing with what I have termed etheric projection.

'I should like to draw the reader's attention particularly to the fact that no wild or preposterous claims are anywhere made in this book,' he wrote, 'as to what has been accomplished during these "astral trips". Mr Muldoon does not claim to have visited any distant planets – and returned to tell us in detail their modes of life; he does not claim to have explored any vast and beautiful "spirit worlds"; he does not pretend to have penetrated the past or the future; to have re-lived any of his past "incarnations"; to have read any "Akashic Records"; to have travelled back along the stream of time and reviewed the history of mankind or the geologic eras of our earth. He asserts merely that he has been enabled to leave his physical body at will and travel about in the present, in his immediate vicinity, in some vehicle or other, while fully conscious.'

Muldoon himself remarked in a letter, 'I have never had a conscious out-of-body experience when I was not here on the earth plane, just as much as I am right now. I wouldn't know where to look for the higher planes!'*

Despite Dr Carrington's difficulties only a year or two before, Sylvan Muldoon was not the only one to claim a detailed knowledge of etheric projection.

The *Occult Review* of 1920 had published two articles on the subject by an engineer named Oliver Fox. Their titles were *The Pineal Doorway* and *Beyond the Pineal Door*. The pineal gland is a small body situated within the brain some distance behind that spot on the forehead where Hindus put the caste mark. Occultists believe it is the remnant of the fabulous Third Eye and the seat of psychical abilities. Scientists are not so sure about the psychical abilities,

---

*Later in this workbook, you will be told where to look for the higher planes if you want to convert an etheric projection into an astral plane projection.

although there is some evidence that the gland remains light sensitive and may be an evolutionary remnant. It secretes a substance called serotonin, which is associated with growth and, just possibly, with visionary experience. For Mr Fox, it was the exit point through which his second body vacated his first.

Around 1902, while Fox was a technical student, he had a spontaneous experience of leaving his physical body. Rather like my own first projection, he found himself standing outside his home. The experience was vivid and real, but there were certain minor changes in his environment that persuaded him he was dreaming. The realization did not cause him to wake up. On the contrary, the 'dream' became more vivid and he was filled by a sensation of well-being. He was so taken by this that he decided to experiment in an effort to bring such dreams under conscious control. His early attempts to do so triggered pain in the pineal area.

With time and practice, he managed to achieve the results he sought and was eventually able to leave his body at will. His experiences thereafter seem to have been a mixture of etheric and astral plane projections.

Carrington himself had discovered yet another source of information by the time he came to edit Muldoon's manuscript. This was the publication, in France, of a book called *Le Fantôme des Vivants* (loosely translated as *The Living Phantom*) by M. Hector Durville. Like Lancelin, Durville was interested in projections resulting from 'magnetic' trances and described a fascinating series of experiments which included attempts to photograph the etheric body. What was happening to these people and to the many others in more recent years who have claimed to be able to separate themselves, more or less at will, from their physical bodies? The first-hand accounts can differ susbstantially, leading to a real degree of confusion among those who approach the literature for the first time.

Look at these two descriptions:

'I dozed off to sleep about ten thirty o'clock . . . and slept for several hours. At length I realized I was slowly awakening, yet I could not seem to drift back into slumber nor further arouse. . .

'Gradually . . . I became more conscious of the fact that I was lying somewhere . . . and shortly I seemed to know that I was reclining upon a bed . . . I tried to move . . . only to find that I was powerless . . . as if adhered to that on which I rested. . . If conscious at the beginning of an exteriorization, one feels fairly glued down, stuck fast, in an immovable position.

'Eventually the feeling of adhesion relaxed, but was replaced by another sensation equally unpleasant – that of floating. . . My entire rigid body – I thought it was my physical, but it was my astral – commenced vibrating at a great rate of speed in an up and down direction and I could feel a tremendous pressure being exerted in the back of my head in the medulla oblongata region. This pressure was very impressive and came in regular spurts, the force of which seemed to pulsate my entire body. . .

'When able to see, I was more than astonished! No words could possibly explain my wonderment. I was floating! I was floating in the very air, rigidly horizontal, a few feet above the bed. . . Slowly, still zigzagging with the strong pressure in the back of my head, I was moved towards the ceiling, all the while horizontal and powerless . . .

'Involuntarily, at about six feet above the bed, as if the movement had been conducted by an invisible force present in the very air, I was uprighted from the horizontal position to the perpendicular and placed standing upon the floor of the room. There I stood for what seemed to me about two minutes, still powerless to move of my own accord, and staring straight ahead . . .

'Then the controlling force relaxed. I felt free, noticing only the tension in the back of my head. I took a step, when the pressure increased for an interval, and threw my body out at an acute angle. I managed to turn round.

'There were two of me! I was beginning to believe myself insane. There was another ''me'' lying quietly upon the bed! It was difficult to convince myself that this was real, but consciousness would not allow me to doubt what I saw.'

This was Sylvan Muldoon's first etheric projection at the age of 12 in a room at the camp of the Mississippi Valley Spiritualists' Association in Clinton, Iowa, where his mother had taken him in an attempt to satisfy her curiosity about spiritualist claims. Bizarre though it is, the account is at least straightforward enough. But contrast it with the following, which is Oliver Fox's description of how he achieved an out-of-body condition:

'I had to force myself through the doorway of the pineal gland . . . It was done, while in the trance condition, simply by concentrating on the pineal gland and willing to ascend through it.

'The sensation was as follows: my incorporeal self rushed to a point in the pineal gland and hurled itself against the imaginary trap-door, while the golden light increased in brilliance so that it seemed the whole room burst into flame.

'If the impetus was insufficient to take me through, then the sensation became reversed; my incorporeal self subsided and became again coincident with my physical body, while the astral light died down to normal.

'Often two or three attempts were required before I could generate sufficient will-power to carry me through. It felt as though I were rushing to insanity and death; but once the little door had clicked behind me, I enjoyed a mental clarity far surpassing that of earth-life. And the fear was gone . . . Leaving the body then was as easy as getting out of bed.

Having left the body, however, Fox's experiences convinced him he was dreaming:

A hundred times would I pass the most glaring incongruities and then at last some inconsistency would tell me that I was dreaming; and always the knowledge brought the change I have described . . . (*An increase in vividness and a sense of well-being* - JHB)

'I found that I was then able to do little tricks at will – levitate, pass through seemingly solid walls, mould matter into new forms etc. . . '

There is so little in common between these accounts that you might be forgiven for imagining they are describing two different experiences. But they are not. Muldoon's account, the first of the two, describes a classical etheric projection, untainted, as Dr Carrington was to point out, with visions of spirit worlds or anything else.

But there is an interesting clue in Fox's account when you come to that phrase 'mould matter into new forms.' This, as you will discover in Section Two, is characteristic of an astral plane projection. Fox, it seems, was one of those individuals whose etheric projections blended into astral plane projections to the confusion of his followers and, I suspect, himself. The breed is by no means rare. Robert Monroe, the American businessman who discovered he had a talent for slipping in and out of his body, soon began to slip between worlds as well. A number of subjects with whom I have experimented using hypnosis as the projection trigger, have tended to do much the same thing. This leads to substantial difficulties in understanding the phenomenon; and even in developing reliable techniques. Before you attempt your own etheric (or, for that matter, astral plane) projections it is as well to have a clear understanding of how the confusion arises. And I think I know.

To talk about projecting a second body (etheric, astral or anything else) is almost certainly in error. When a projection occurs, what leaves the physical is not a single subtle body, but a collection of them. Think back to that Russian dolls analogy. When you take the first doll from the outer case, you automatically take the whole series of inner dolls along with it.

As you will discover in Section Two of the workbook, astral plane projection also involves a subtle body. Not, I believe, the etheric, but something even more tenuous than an energy field, a body which occultists think of as composed of 'mind stuff' – the true astral body. When all your various bodies coincide – as is the case throughout most of your waking day – they hold together tenaciously and spontaneous projection rarely occurs. Once you separate the subtle bodies from the physical, however, there is a breakdown in the tenacity of the system. This is a long-winded way of saying that when you project the etheric body (with its coincident astral, mental and spiritual bodies) there is at least a possibility, and perhaps even a tendency, for the innermost bodies – i.e. the astral/mental/spiritual complex – to project spontaneously. Thus, from a straightforward etheric projection such as Sylvan Muldoon invariably experienced, you *may* find yourself slipping into the Astral World as has been the experience of Fox, Monroe and others.

The position could actually be even more complicated than that. There is a case to be made for the possibility that your astral, mental and spiritual bodies

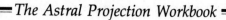

are *already* separated and active within their own inner worlds. According to this theory, what really projects is not a body at all, but your focus of consciousness. My own experiments have left me in considerable sympathy with this idea. If you find it difficult to follow at this stage, don't lose too much sleep – it should become much clearer once you have worked your way through the second section of this book.

For now, it is of little importance which theory is correct, since neither is involved in the practicalities of projection. But before getting down to those, it is as well for you to know what you are getting into when you do leave your body.

3.

The Silver Cord

Your projected etheric body feels very like the old familiar corpse you carry round each day. 'I thought it was my physical, but it was my astral,' wrote Sylvan Muldoon in the account I have already quoted. And again: 'I believed naturally that this was my physical body, as I had always known it, but that it had mysteriously begun to defy gravity. It was too unnatural for me to understand, yet too real to deny . . .'

This ease of confusion between physical and etheric is further emphasized by an early personal experience of my own which I have recounted elsewhere, but nonetheless bears repeating here. I awoke in the night with a need to urinate. I climbed out of bed, walked across the room and found the bedroom door not only closed, but locked. I could not understand this, but neither could I open the door. It was only after a few moments that I realized my hand was actually *sinking into* the handle.

I returned to the bed and discovered my (physical) body still lying there beside my wife. I climbed back, realigned myself, and sank back into coincidence with the physical, then headed for the bathroom again. Once again I reached the door; and once again I found I had left my physical body behind. I returned to the bed; in fact I had to return to the bed several more times before I could persuade my physical body to come with me and open the door.

Although the incident was trivial, it was also highly instructive. The first thing that strikes me, looking back, is that I had left the bed, crossed the bedroom, and stood at the door for several moments *before it occurred to me that I was not in my normal physical body*. This is an important point. Given that we are discussing a field of electrical energy (or at most a lump of matter weighing $2\frac{1}{2}$ ozs) you would certainly be entitled to imagine it must *feel* different. Yet it does not. Subjectively, you can scarcely tell the difference. I felt I had my normal weight. I seemed subject to gravity. I felt the chill in the air and was still aware of the pressure in my bladder.

My physical environment – the bedroom walls, the furnishings, the door – all *looked* perfectly solid and normal, although as I discovered with the handle (and later, when I passed completely through a closed door) I could not touch them in the normal way, nor could I *feel* them. The effect was rather like walking through a life-size hologram. But there was one exception to the general rule: I could feel the carpet beneath my feet. The reason for all this may be the way the human mind works. It seems safe to assume that if you spend a lifetime operating in a physical body, you develop deeply ingrained habits associated with it; including habits of perception.

Most psychologists are convinced that what you see is conditioned by what you expect to see. For example, one interesting experiment has indicated that our ability to judge the length of lines is influenced by social factors. If enough of your companions insist the shorter line is longer, that is the way you will come to see it.

The act of walking includes a multitude of subtle sensations, among them your perception of balance, the feel of the terrain beneath your feet, the length of each step . . . and so on, combining into a continual feedback which enables you to get on with your stroll while discussing the weather. Most of the feedback is quite unconscious. Indeed the act of walking hardly impinges at all until you get pain signals associated with tired muscles or a stone in the shoe. Walking over rough, unfamiliar terrain, I might have had to pay attention. Walking across the floor of the bedroom in which I had slept for years, everything went on automatic. I expected the feel of the carpet beneath my feet; and even in my etheric body, that is exactly what I got. In other words, the feel of the carpet was, within the framework of the incident I described, a hallucination.

If this sounds unlikely, it is as well to remember that Carl Jung, a practising psychiatrist and one of the founding fathers of modern psychology, insisted hallucinations are far more widespread than people imagine. The problem is, we tend only to doubt our perceptions if they are bizarre. Thus, if you walk into a room and find it occupied by a little green man in a flying saucer, you will probably feel at least a twinge of doubt. But the ashtray lying on the table next to him could equally well be a hallucination – and one that would never be challenged unless you actually tried to touch it.

If the sensation of the carpet beneath my feet was no more than a habit response, the desire to urinate was in a different category. This desire – which I continued to experience while in my etheric body – is known to be a response to a purely *physical* trigger mechanism: pressure on the bladder. Since we have already noted the etheric body forms a pattern for the physical rather than a reflection of it, we can assume expansion of the physical bladder does not change its etheric counterpart. We can also assume that since the desire to urinate is (hopefully) an intermittent phenomenon, it would not create the same conditioned response as walking on a familiar carpet. In these circumstances, we are left with a mystery. How did I (and other projectors, incidentally) experience full-bladder pressure in a body lacking a full bladder?

The most likely answer, of course, was that I was continuing to experience the pressure felt by my *physical* body – something that requires a communications link between the two. I have never been personally aware of such a link in any etheric projection, but Mr Muldoon has. He saw it as a sort of cord or cable:

'My two identical bodies were joined by an elastic-like cable, one end of which was fastened to the *medulla oblongata* region of the astral counter-part, while the other centred between the eyes of the physical counterpart. This cable extended across the space of probably six feet which separated us.'

Muldoon's 'cable' is one of the most interesting aspects of etheric projection. It is mentioned in the records of many other projectors, yet some, like myself, have managed to leave the body without ever noticing it. And where it does appear, it breaks a lot of rules. The cable seems to be the same thing as the 'silver cord' mentioned in the Bible which, according to these scriptures, snaps on death. But failing death, nothing seems to bother it much. If Arthur Gibson's experience was anything to go by, it will obligingly stretch all the way from Ireland to the Indian sub-continent. And even this does not define the extent of its elasticity, for some projectors have reported trips off the planet during which the cord thinned a little, but did not break. Nor does it tangle. This may not appear particularly surprising, since the cord, like the remainder of the etheric body, passes through physical objects. But even when two or more subjects project simultaneously, there never seems to be any problem with these trailing cords.

I suspect that useful though it may be in some respects, the analogy of an infinitely elastic cable is not entirely accurate. What is perceived as a cord seems to be no more than the subjective impression of a definite link – and an impression, moreover, that is not always present. If this is correct, it is the link that is important, not whether there is a literal cord. The existence of such a link seems almost beyond argument and means that certain physical sensations (such as my now-famous full bladder) can be transmitted to the etheric body, which experiences them – more or less – as its own.

This linkage is the reason why occultists have long cautioned against any interference with the physical body of a subject who is in the projected state. Even a light touch is sufficient to alert the phantom which instinctively jerks back to its physical shell from whatever distance it is separated. I have experienced this phenomenon – which is sometimes accompanied by a subjective clanging sound, like metal striking metal – and can assure you it is something to be avoided. Although it has never seemed to do me any great harm, esoteric literature is full of warnings that it can trigger serious health conditions up to and including strokes and heart attacks. Certainly it is extremely unpleasant.

Communication between physical and phantom is a two-way process. That is to say, trauma suffered in the etheric body can be transmitted back to the physical double. Several years ago, Marvel Comics published an engaging fantasy in which Dr Strange ('Master of the Mystic Arts') was attacked by the phantom of a rival wizard while in the course of an etheric projection. Someone at Marvel must have undertaken in-depth research, for Dr Strange's phantom was joined to his physical body by a cable such as Muldoon describes . . . which his rival was attempting to cut with an astral knife. While this sort of thing is great fun, it bears little resemblance to real life. But the principle behind the attack on Dr Strange's phantom is sound enough: harm the etheric and you will harm the physical. Unless you find yourself in very peculiar circumstances, the worst physical discomfort you are likely to suffer is a headache, but there is a possibility of picking up a few bruises, the origins of which are not entirely obvious.

The existence of a link permits the phantom to control the physical body – after a fashion – at a distance. During one series of projections, I would typically find myself floating no more than a foot or so above my physical body which I could move (with some difficulty) and through which I could speak. The sensation was very peculiar, like manipulating a marionette with strings.

The link, or cord, maintains a light pull on the phantom throughout the projection; and as Sylvan Muldoon noted, approaching too close to the physical causes the pull to increase. Once a critical point has been passed, which varies a little from subject to subject, but is usually no more than a few feet, the action of the cord draws the phantom suddenly back into the physical. This effect makes it very difficult to examine your physical body from close range while exteriorized.

If nothing else, the discovery provides some much-needed reassurance for inexperienced projectors, whose most common question is, 'What happens if I can't get back into my (physical) body?' Almost every account insists, with Muldoon, that the problem is not getting back in, but managing to stay out – especially if you approach too closely to the physical.

A related effect gives an equally reassuring answer to 'What happens if I travel so far in my etheric body that I get lost and can't find my way back?' If you are aware of the cable, you can reel yourself in like a fish; or follow it along like Ariadne's thread in the Minotaur's labyrinth. If you are not, then there is still little cause for concern, for etheric trips are self-limiting. Once your physical body becomes uncomfortable, or hungry, as it is bound to do eventually, the sensation of 'pull' grows progressively stronger until it is irresistible. If you cannot wait, Robert Monroe advises simply thinking about some body part and attempting to move it (e.g. wiggling the big toe.) This, he says, is sufficient to bring you back to the physical instantaneously.

If you remain outside your physical body for any length of time, several interesting differences between the experience and your normal mode of physical operation become noticeable.

The most dramatic is, of course, the ability to pass through solid objects. Robert Monroe, the American businessman who later became a highly experienced projector, tells how this particular ability gave him an early indication that what was happening to him was not some sort of illness.

Monroe had a very hard time with his first projection. Long before it occurred, he began to experience painful cramps and rigidity of the upper abdomen. This was followed, over a period of weeks, by bouts of temporary paralysis during which his entire body would seem to shake violently, like one in the grip of malaria. (The sensation was subjective – no shaking of the physical body actually occurred.)

'Within the following six weeks,' Monroe wrote, 'the same peculiar condition manifested itself nine times. It occurred at different periods and locales, and the only common factor was that it began just after I had lain down for a rest or sleep. Whenever it took place, I fought myself to a sitting position and the ''shaking'' faded away. . . '

Like the doctor of my young visitor, Monroe considered the possibility of epilepsy, but dismissed it on the grounds that epileptics had no memory of their seizures while his own recollection of the experience was clear. He suspected a brain disorder, possibly a tumor, and sought medical advice. His doctor suggested he was simply working too hard and should lose a little weight.

Monroe's 'symptoms' continued to recur and, as happens in such cases, his initial fear died down until eventually he came to find the experience almost boring. When the 'vibrations', as he called them, struck, he would simply wait patiently for them to pass. On one occasion as he did so, his arm was draped over the side of the bed, his fingers just brushing the rug.

'Idly, I tried to move my fingers and found I could scratch the rug. Without thinking or realizing that I *could* move my fingers during the vibration, I pushed with the tips of my fingers against the rug. After a moment's resistance, my fingers seemed to penetrate the rug and touch the floor underneath. With mild curiosity, I pushed my hand down further. My fingers went through the floor and there was the rough upper surface of the ceiling of the room below . . . I was surely wide awake and the sensation was still there. How could I be awake in all other respects and still ''dream'' that my arm was stuck down through the floor?'

But arms stuck through floors or, as in my own case, hands sinking into doorknobs are not the only peculiarities of the projected state. There is, for example, a slightly different quality about the light, which seems curiously flat. Although Oliver Fox spoke of a golden glow, this seems to have been an intrusion from the Astral Plane and is not something generally experienced by etheric projectors. Many, in fact, report no peculiarities about the light at all – which is not surprising since the difference is not so pronounced as to be particularly noticeable.

What *is* very noticeable once it starts to manifest is the way the etheric body gets about. Muldoon chronicled three 'movement speeds', each of which coincides with my own experience. The first is the old familiar walking pace. When I moved from my bed to the door, I did so exactly as I would have in the physical body. And later, I strolled across other rooms and walked downstairs in exactly the same way.

The second, which Muldoon describes as 'intermediate speed', is substantially faster and is associated with a phenomenon that has no physical counterpart – at least for ordinary mortals. This speed is roughly equivalent to travelling on the back of a fast horse, or driving in a car. The phenomenon with which it is associated is levitation.

Levitation has already been mentioned, although not by name, in one of Muldoon's quoted accounts. You may recall that, during his first projection, he found himself *floating* above his physical body in a state of paralysis before some process set him upright. I have had the same sensation of floating a foot or two above my physical body in minor projection experiences, but more to the present point, I noticed that when climbing or descending stairs during an exteriorization, my feet were actually some inches *above* the treads. This is relevant to Muldoon's intermediate speed of travel in the etheric, for my own experience strongly suggests this mode of movement involves levitation. You rush along at a very satisfying rate *with your feet some distance off the ground.* Even more bizarre reports of projectors who have travelled into space indicates that levitation in the etheric body may be pushed to extremes.

The third speed listed by Muldoon is not really a speed at all, but a sort of instantaneous travel which has no physical counterpart at all, outside of science fiction. It is easy enough to describe. You *think* yourself towards your destination and, when you get the knack, you are instantly there.

There is no sensation of movement. Muldoon believed the mind could not cope with the speeds involved and momentarily blacked out, but I doubt this to be the case. It seems to me that neither speed nor motion is actually involved here, but rather a different *principle* of transportation which allows instantaneous transfer from one location to another. Certainly there is no sensation of elapsed time and distance does not seem to be any object.

So long as you avoid slipping into an astral plane projection, the information you have already absorbed should permit you to function with a reasonable degree of confidence when you find yourself out of the body. But at this stage of the workbook, having covered such oddities as walking through walls, levitation and instantaneous travel, two questions obviously arise: is it for real . . . and is it safe?

Both deserve honest answers before embarking on a study of the techniques which will allow you to duplicate the feats of Fox, Muldoon, Monroe and others.

4.

Dangers of Projection

Robert Allen Monroe studied commerce, engineering, journalism and drama at Ohio State University. In 1937, he went into broadcasting as a writer/director. He moved to New York, where he made his living writing features and screenplays before breaking into network radio with a long-running dramatized documentary. At the end of World War II, he formed his own production company and embarked on a highly successful business career. In 1958, he experienced his first etheric projection.

In 1986, Souvenir Press in Britain published *Far Journeys*, his second book on the subject. It opened with these words:

'If there is a first and obvious point to be made, I can report that I am still alive physically after 25 years of exploring personally the out-of-body experience. A little time-worn, but still more or less operational.

'There were several moments when I was not so sure. However, some of the best medical authorities have assured me that the physical problems I have encountered have been simply cause and effect of living in the culture/civilization of mid-twentieth century America. Some take another position. I am still alive as a *result* of such OBE activity. Take your pick.

'So it would seem that one can practice ''going out of the body'' regularly and survive. Also, after having been tested periodically by experts, I can still make the statement that I am reasonably sane . . . '

Although lightly put, this is a point of considerable importance. Giving up the ghost is so firmly associated with death in many cultures that it is only reasonable to ask if temporary separations are safe. Monroe has given his answer: he is neither dead nor mad after quarter of a century of practice. It is an answer which seems to be borne out by others.

Sylvan Muldoon was a very sick man when he first contacted Dr Carrington. 'I wish I could have felt better when I was writing this book,' he was quoted as saying, 'for I probably could have done a better job. As it is, every word was written with reluctance.' Some words were, in fact, written while he was too ill to get out of bed. During this period, Muldoon projected frequently without managing to kill himself, despite his severely weakened condition. Indeed, he formed a theory that his illness actually *aided* his projective abilities. He thought it somehow loosened his etheric body.

If projection is unlikely to kill you, are there any other safety problems? The question of getting back in to your body has already been covered (follow the cord or wiggle your big toe) and seems to cause little difficulty. Monroe once found himself getting into the *wrong* body – the only time I have ever heard of this happening – but says that the 'wiggling the big toe' technique will sort this out as well.

Can someone, or some*thing*, get into *your* body while you are away? Although Monroe's experience of mistakenly trying to get into the wrong body must suggest this is just possible, it does not appear to be very likely. 'Over the past 15 years, working with laboratory subjects and program participants, there have been no incidents that could remotely be construed as ''possession'' or something destructive or uncontrollable,' he states categorically.

I can find nothing in the published literature to suggest that an out-of-body experience is any more dangerous than crossing the road . . . and may be considerably less so. Neither my considerable personal experience with projectors nor my considerably less personal experience with projection has led me to believe otherwise. The worst that seems to happen is the occasional headache, minor pain or stiffness – and Monroe claims these are no more than the result of unconscious anxieties and will disappear once you come to terms with your natural fears about projection.

Some projectors are convinced everyone has the ability to leave the body with a little training and effort. Muldoon and one or two others go even further, suggesting that projection is a natural function which you *already experience* whether you realize it or not. According to this theory, your etheric body slips out of coincidence with the physical body during sleep, a process which allows you to recharge with vital energy.

But if projection seems to be safe, it is not always pleasant. Sometimes it can be very unpleasant indeed. That slight slippage, which Muldoon says occurs naturally during sleep, can cause disorientation, balance problems and a sensation of illness if it happens while you are wide awake. (These symptoms are indicative of a number of conditions, but if you suspect etheric slippage, firm pressure on the top of the head, at a point midway between an imaginary line drawn to link the tips of the ears, will usually put it right.)

Another familiar example of partial spontaneous projection is the jolt sensation many people experience when falling asleep, especially if overly tired. Typically this arises after an exhausting day when you lie down desperate for sleep, but cannot stop your mind going over the events of the day. In these circumstances, beginning to drift often results in a violent jolting sensation which brings you wide awake again. This sensation, says Dr Douglas Baker, results from the double slipping out of the physical, then jerking back in again. In a straw poll taken at his lectures on the subject, he discovered some 60 per cent of his audiences had experienced the sensation. Since I find myself among them, I can attest it is something I would prefer to avoid.

First indication of a full projection is often paralysis of the entire body – what

Muldoon terms catalepsy or the 'glued-down' feeling. A writer colleague of mine triggered the cataleptic state while attempting to stimulate a projection and told me later it was one of the most unpleasant and frightening experiences he had ever had. Most people react to the sensation with distate, unease, fear or even panic – especially if they have not been warned about the possibility in advance.

The 'shaking' or 'vibration' mentioned by Robert Monroe is by no means uncommon either; and is again almost universally experienced as unpleasant. Part of the problem is lack of control. When paralysis or vibration begin, it requires an enormous effort to break free of them – and in some instances you are powerless to break free at all and can only wait for the condition to pass. Another part is the fact that these experiences feel like the symptoms of illness – and a serious illness at that. Even when warned in advance about the possibility of their occurrence, you tend to lie in their grip wondering if this is *really* the start of a projection or if, coincidentally, you are suffering from a heart attack or stroke.

It would be unfair to overstress these negative factors. My own few projections have been trouble free; and one of the best projectors I know claims that the whole process is only a matter of 'letting go', which she does with such expertise that she can now step in and out of the body at will, with no catalepsy, vibration, or any other symptoms whatsoever. But it is certain that some projectors do have problems. And if forewarning about the symptoms does not make them any more pleasant, it may perhaps provide some small reassurance until you grow accustomed to them . . . or learn how to avoid them altogether.

If the question of safety is relatively easy to answer, the question of *reality* has proven more difficult. Certainly there is *something* peculiar going on. Even if I had not experienced the phenomenon for myself, I would still be quite satisfied that projectors are undergoing an extraordinary experience, if only because the brain's electrical patterns change dramatically during a projection. In one series of experiments, for example, I was able to monitor the brain waves of a subject projecting with the aid of induced hypnotic trance. The read-out first showed the alpha rhythm typical of hypnosis, then a sharp jump in intensity at the moment of projection. Thereafter, it was actually possible to 'track' the progress of the etheric body around the room, since the brainwaves varied in intensity in relation to the subject's perceived (out-of-body) position.

Dr Charles T. Tart has reported substantially more sophisticated tests on Robert Monroe during the period September 1965 to August 1966, using the facilities of the Electroencephalographic Laboratory of the University of Virginia Medical School. During these experiments, Monroe's brainwaves, heart rate and eye movements were all monitored during projection. The tests typically indicated brainwave patterns associated with dreaming sleep and were usually accompanied by rapid eye movements, also associated with dreaming. His heart rate remained within its normal 65 to 70 beats per minute range, but during some of the sessions, his blood pressure showed a sudden drop, a steady low (apparently during the period he was out of the body) followed by a sudden resurgence to normal.

A little over a decade later, Monroe underwent further tests at the hands of Drs Stuart Twemlow and Fowler Jones at the University of Kansas Medical Centre, using left and right occipital electoencephalograph readings and a Beckman polygraph. (The latter is commonly called a 'lie-detector' but is actually used to measure a variety of physical functions such as galvanic skin reponse, temperature variations and blood pressure fluctuations.)

The EEG tests generally tended to confirm Tart's findings that Monroe projected in a state very similar, if not identical, to light (dreaming) sleep. There was, however, a 'dramatic reduction in neuronal energy in the alpha and theta band' – quite the reverse of my own findings with a hypnotized subject. There was also, reported Twemlow and Jones, 'some unusual patterns *not* characteristic of REM (rapid eye movement or dream) sleep or other normal sleep stages.'

The polygraph produced even more interesting readings. Galvanic skin response showed an arousal increase of some 150 microvolts when the sessions began, but no response whatsoever during Monroe's projections.

To confuse the picture even further, Tart reported that an unnamed 'young lady' whose out-of-body experiences were accidental, but frequent, showed a different brainwave pattern to Monroe, without, however, indicating exactly what.

Clearly, the monitoring of subjects' bodies shows physiological responses which would be difficult, if not impossible, to fake, coincident with the subjective experience of projection. But those responses do not form a coherent pattern; and vary from subject to subject. It would appear that projection causes definite physical reactions, but these reactions differ depending on the state you are in to begin with.

Experiments of this type are all very well and doubtless important within their own frame of reference, but whatever brainwave patterns and GSR manifest, they do no more than tell us that subjects who claim to project are unlikely to be lying through their teeth. They give no guarantee that projections have any objective validity. Indeed the REM state Stage 1 sleep pattern which showed in the Monroe experiments might be taken to indicate he was only dreaming.

Certainly, not every scientist who investigated him was prepared to accept the *objective* nature of projection. One paper issued by Drs Twemlow and Glen O. Gabbard begins with a rather unsympathetic analysis of Monroe's personality traits. According to the good doctors these include potential areas of conflict in the realms of sexuality, aggression and depression. They go on to relate his out-of-body trips with 'a grandiose fantasy' known as 'the Dædalus Experience'. This psychological condition, named after the Greek who flew too near the sun, typically appears in childhood, but does not always disappear later.

'The fascination with out-of-body ''travel'' seen in Monroe is likely an adult derivative of this Dædalus fantasy,' wrote Twemlow and Gabbard, who later concluded, 'Thus, the out-of-body experience in Monroe also serves the function of avoidance of conflict. By transcending the prison of his body, it allows him to steer clear of such potential conflict areas as sexuality, depression and aggression.' In short, Monroe's projections are presented as an hysterical reaction to an essentially neurotic condition.

If Monroe himself is disturbed by this sort of twaddle, he may draw some consolation from the fact that among others believed to suffer from the Dædalus fantasy were Tolstoy and Sir Winston Churchill. Furthermore, if Dædalus is the dynamic behind projection, the fantasy is uncommonly wide-spread. A 1954 student survey showed 27.1 per cent of respondents had had an out-of-body experience, the majority of them more than once. Celia Green's study of Oxford undergraduates in 1968 showed an even higher figure (34 per cent). Both surveys were conducted on a small, selective base, but in 1975 a far wider sampling was taken. This showed a 25 per cent rate of OOB experience among students and a 14 per cent rate among the general population. Even these figures may only be the tip of an iceberg. When, in 1976, a mass circulation North American publication appealed for information on the subject, 700 out of 1,500 replies claimed out-of-body experiences – a staggering 46.6 per cent.

Does this only mean a great many of us are off our heads . . . or is there a real possibility that the subjective experience of leaving the body is no less than the literal truth? Some 94 per cent of those interviewed claim the experience to be 'more real than a dream'. What evidence is there that they might be right?

Let me start close to home with Arthur Gibson, the projector, you may recall, who managed to stretch his astral cord to India. Arthur's report of Bombay was vivid, detailed, but hardly evidential since he had lived and worked in that city for many years. But among all the familiar sights, Arthur discovered two that were entirely unexpected. In the old quarter of the city was a newly-built wall where none had been before; and his favourite restaurant had been redecorated. Arthur checked with a friend still living in Bombay and found both these perceptions had been correct. In a more controllable experiment, I hypnotized Arthur and had him project into the house next door, which he had never physically entered. He was able to describe its layout, rooms, decor and furnishings accurately, in considerable detail and with little apparent difficulty.

A similar sort of experiment was carried out with the help of a teenage shop assistant named Denise Alexander who was persuaded, again under hypnosis, to project from a site near Kill, in County Kildare in the Republic of Ireland to a house in Lisburn, County Antrim in Northern Ireland – a distance of some 100 miles. Waiting for her on the mantlepiece of the living room in the Lisburn house was a short note, the contents of which was known only to two colleagues who, having left it there, took no further part in the experiment. (And were actually out of the country on holiday when it took place.) Denise failed to read the note – she said she found the room too dark – but was able to report (accurately) that it was block printed on unlined blue paper and contained exactly five words.

Both these experiments were originally published in my book *Astral Doorways* as long ago as 1971. Since then, I have had little difficulty in persuading a variety of subjects to report back accurately on scenes, people and things they have seen while out of the body. There are only a limited number of explanations for this accuracy if you are prepared to accept that fraud played no part in the experiments. Telepathy is one. Clairvoyance – a direct perception of distant events – is another. And actual projection is a third.

It is difficult to see how telepathy played any part in Arthur Gibson's Bombay trip, since no one else present had ever visited the city or was particularly interested in it. The experiment with Denise Alexander was specifically structured to avoid the possibility of telepathy, since the only people who knew the contents of the note were at the time in an unknown location.

Clairvoyance is a lot more difficult. I am fairly happy (for reasons which need not concern us here) that it is possible for some people to obtain information at a distance without leaving the body. (And an aspect of the training outlined in Part Two of this workbook tends, coincidentally, to stimulate this faculty.) But the *subjective* experience of so doing is very different from projection. If we insist on clairvoyance as the answer, we have to insist on clairvoyance simultaneously and coincidentally accompanied by a vivid, associated hallucination . . . something I frankly find difficult to swallow.

Americans have a colourful saying to the effect that 'if it walks like a duck and quacks like a duck, chances are it really is a duck.' I tend to believe the experiments I have carried out in this field walk like ducks and point to the fact that their subjects really have projected. But there was one (perhaps important) flaw in my method. Without exception, the projections I initiated involved hypnosis. Since hypnosis can easily produce vivid hallucinations, it becomes possible to argue that the phenomenon was one of trance rather than projection. Fortunately the pointers towards genuine projection do not end with my poor efforts.

Tart, for example, required one of his subjects (the same 'young lady' who produced brainwave patterns different from Monroe's) to read a target number located in a room different from that in which she projected. She did so successfully. While unable to read the target number, Monroe himself successfully reported finding a laboratory assistant and her husband in the target room.

Hereward Carrington went one better. Possibly encouraged by the activities of his star subject, Sylvan Muldoon, Carrington willed himself to project into the presence of 'a certain young lady' who had a reputation as a psychic. This is the sort of thing most of us (men) would quite like to be able to do, but Carrington's attempts produced none of the conscious projections of Muldoon and were consequently judged a failure . . . until, that is, the lady in question reported waking to find him standing in her room or sitting on her bed at the time he was attempting his projections. He remained for a few moments before fading away.

While this sort of case is interesting, it raises more questions than it answers – notably how Carrington could have projected so successfully without being aware of it. But unconscious projection may be far more common than many scientists imagine; as are instances of people catching sight of the ghostly bodies of projectors. In January 1957, for example, an American woman, Martha Johnson, projected from Plains, Illinois in the early hours of the morning in order to visit her mother almost a thousand miles away in northern Minnesota. She succeeded in the experiment and found her mother at work in the kitchen. Ms Johnson leaned against the dish cupboard and watched. Eventually her mother grew disturbed and turned to look at her. Ms Johnson experienced an understandable feeling of satisfaction and left.

The following day, Martha's mother wrote a letter which said in part:

'It would have been about ten after two, your time. (*Ms Johnson projected a little after 2. a.m.* – JHB) I was pressing a blouse here in the kitchen. I looked up and there you were at the cupboard just standing smiling at me. I started to speak to you and you were gone. I forgot for a moment where I was. I think the dogs saw you too. They got so excited.'

Scientists fight very shy of this sort of evidence, which is categorized as 'anecdotal', a label which often allows it to be conveniently ignored. But if you experience projection and can tell what I am doing, while I in turn can see your phantom body in my room, I would venture to suggest once again the whole thing walks like a duck. Modern psychical research is plagued by a sort of paranoid scepticism among the scientific establishment which attempts to force stronger and stronger evidence, tighter and tighter controls, far beyond what would be accepted in any other discipline.

Something of the same attitude has rubbed off onto paranormal investigators themselves, who will often create the most tortuous theories to explain (or explain away) phenomena, the explanation of which is plainly presented by the phenomena itself. On my reading of the evidence, there is little doubt that projection of the phantom actually occurs, that you can travel within it to distant parts, that you can bring back accurate news and that, sometimes, you can actually be seen. But for those of you who want just a little more, consider the case of Stuart Blue Harary.

Stuart Blue Harary is another of those projectors who have co-operated with science in an attempt to find out what on earth is going on when they exercise their talent. In this instance, the site of the experiments was Duke University of North Carolina, perhaps best known as the place where Dr J.B. Rhine first established his statistical ESP card-calling experiments.

Harary's experiments were substantially more complex. His pulse, blood pressure, galvanic skin response, breathing, eye movements and brainwaves were all monitored. A target room approximately half a mile away was packed with thermistors, photo multipliers and various devices for measuring electrical conductivity and magnetic permeability. When Harary projected, his heartbeat and respiration increased and blood pressure dropped. There was a similar decrease in galvanic skin response. Some rapid eye movements were noted, but he was not asleep, since the EEG showed a steady alpha rhythm, associated with relaxed alertness.

Scientists monitoring the various instruments in the target lab subsequently reported Harary had failed to influence any of them . . . except one. Among the mechanical devices was a confined kitten, appropriately named *Spirit*. Harary had been instructed to soothe it by stroking if he was successful in visiting the lab. Spirit mewed 37 times during a control period, but not at all during the two two-minute periods when Harary reported stroking it while he was out of the body.

This is a fascinating instance of the correct choice of detection equipment, for cats have long been believed to have the ability to see ghosts. I have owned several myself who were always doing it.

5.

What Helps You Leave Your Body

But how do you do it?

Assuming you are not among the few who have experienced spontaneous projection, or the fewer still who have experienced it more than once, how do you roll out of your body to walk around like a ghost, passing through walls, visiting young ladies in their chambers and generally behaving in a reprehensible manner?

In 1977, two multiscale questionnaires delightfully named POBE and PAL were dispatched to some 700 Americans who had reported out-of-body experiences. POBE stood for Profile of the Out-of-Body Experience; PAL was Profile of Adaption to Life, a measure of psychological health; and just possibly an unconscious measure of how the investigating scientist viewed individuals who claimed to have left their bodies. The survey elicited 339 replies and analysis of respondents' answers produced an interesting ranking of what might be called pre-existent conditions – what, in other words, the situation was immediately before projection happened.

The authors of the survey, our old friends Drs Twemlow, Gabbard and Jones, expressed the following caveat: 'Of course, no cause-effect relationship necessarily occurs between these conditions and the experience itself, although such has been implied by a number of authors.' I fear I am about to make such an implication myself, for my experience suggests that those who train themselves to bring about certain of the pre-existent conditions have a far better chance of projecting than those who do not. But what are the conditions?

Some, admittedly, are hardly relevant to training. Five per cent, for example, projected following cardiac arrest. Ten per cent were near death from other causes. Three per cent had high fever, four per cent had just suffered an accident, while a further four per cent left their bodies during childbirth. (This last is interesting, since it obviously relates only to female respondents, who comprised 52 per cent of the sample. It is not clear if the 4 per cent figure is quoted in relation only to females or to the survey as a whole. If to the survey as a whole, it indicates a surprisingly high incidence of projection during childbirth – almost one in ten among susceptible subjects.) We might also safely ignore the 2 per cent of projections which occurred while driving a vehicle. When asked his advice about what to do if you found yourself in this position,

Robert Monroe answered wisely, 'Get back as fast as you can!'

But even leaving all these aside, there are still a great many areas which may repay closer examination. Top of the list, present in some 79 per cent of cases, was the fact that the subject was *physically relaxed*. In all the projections I have induced by hypnosis, deep relaxation has been a characteristic. It was also present, without exception, in my own spontaneous projections. One analytical projector of considerable experience, has made the interesting suggestion that projection is not a matter of *driving* the etheric body out of the physical body, but rather of *letting it go*. If this is correct, then relaxation, which is itself a matter of 'letting go', is an obvious aid to the process.

Drugs can sometimes be of assistance. While under medical treatment I experienced a whole series of projections triggered by injections of a powerful muscle relaxant. General anaesthetic, which now almost always involves the use of muscle relaxants, was a pre-existent condition in 6 per cent of surveyed cases. Even tranquilizers can help: some of my early projections occurred while I was enjoying the benefits of librium. But these are all drugs which require medical supervision and are thus more likely to trigger accidental projections than form part of a structured training programme. The most commonly available social drug – alcohol – although a relaxant and depressant, does not appear to be particularly conducive to projection: it is listed as a factor in only two per cent of cases. The problem seems to be the way alcohol reacts on the nervous system. By releasing inhibitions, it generates euphoria. Relaxation does follow, but as deep muscular relaxation is achieved, reflexes are depressed, co-ordination ruined, speech slurred and mentation profoundly affected. In other words, by the time you are relaxed enough to project, you are usually too drunk to care.

There is some evidence that hallucinogenic drugs, including anything but very small quantities of cannabis, can induce projection, but at the cost of control. In one experiment, for example, the subject triggered projections by smoking fairly heavy concentrations of cannabis resin, only to spend two hours swinging uncontrollably in and out of his body like a pendulum. Fortunately there are several safer, and more legal, ways to achieve deep muscular relaxation. One already mentioned is hypnosis.

Although my own experiments have used hypnosis to trigger projections directly, this is not what I am advocating here. For many people, hypnosis is an exceptional tool for inducing a totally relaxed state. Having achieved that state, you can then go on to apply the various other techniques which will help you achieve projection. But first find your hypnotist. You might, of course, quite literally do just that. Most cities and quite a few large towns support one or two professional hypnotherapists. Search the yellow pages or the advertising columns of the evening paper and when you find one whose approach and credentials satisfy you, make an appointment. Say you suffer from a tension problem – which is probably true even if you do not realize it – and want to be trained in relaxation. Typically you will be expected to pay by the session, each of which will last about an hour. For commonplace problems like smoking or tension, some hypnotherapists are prepared to conduct group sessions which cut down on costs.

If you would prefer not to attend a hypnotist, or simply cannot find one in your area, you can always import one into your own home through the medium of a cassette tape. There are a great many hypnotic induction tapes on the market*, usually available for little more than the price of a paperback book. Although you can pick one that simply promises relaxation, my advice would be to go for one that trains you in self-hypnosis, a truly invaluable skill once you get the knack.

For those nervous of hypnosis – and they are legion – biofeedback training is a possibility. Biofeedback training is based on the interesting notion that none of us are stupid: once we are shown how to do something, we can usually manage it a second time.

A great many physical processes – your heart rate, for example, or the amount of acid secreted by your stomach in response to a barbecued spare rib – are not under conscious control. But they can be *brought* under conscious control through training. Equipment which monitors these processes, then signals them either audibly or visually, allows this to happen. Once you can *see* or *hear* when your body is doing something, you can usually take conscious charge of the process after relatively few practice sessions.

Muscular tension is not entirely an unconscious activity – you can flex and relax your biceps any time you choose – but for a great many people, it has an unconscious *component.* How often have you found yourself frowning, gritting your teeth, hunching your shoulders, or tensing your stomach muscles without realizing you were doing it? Biofeedback training makes you aware of these unconscious or semi-conscious tensions so that you can do something about them. There are various indicators of muscular tension. Perhaps the simplest is one we have already encountered: galvanic skin response. The more relaxed you become, the lower the electrical resistance of your skin. While highly sensitive, complex and expensive GSR machines exist, it is perfectly possible to monitor this response using a hand-held device little larger than a packet of cigarettes. An audible tone drops in pitch as you begin to relax, allowing you to relax even further.

This and several other biofeedback devices are obtainable, in the United Kingdom, from Aleph One Ltd., of The Old Courthouse, Bottisham, Cambridge CB5 9BA, England. Current lists and costings may be had by writing to this address or phoning 0223-811679.

If you prefer to avoid anything fancy, you can always train yourself in muscular relaxation the hard way – by sheer, dogged practice. This is, I suppose, where the *work* part of the workbook really begins. Starting tomorrow morning and continuing each morning thereafter, I would like you to set aside a short period for the practice of relaxation.

How much time you spend is up to you but you will find anything less than 10

---

*Thorsons Publishing Group sells a comprehensive selection by mail. Catalogues are free from the Group at Denington Estate, Wellingborough, Northants, NN8 2RQ, England.

minutes is useless. If you are going to take projection seriously, I would suggest half an hour; and strongly suggest you make the practice a habit, because continuity of effort is important.

You will need privacy. This is one reason for selecting morning time – if you get up early enough, nobody else will be about. Try and find a place where you will not be disturbed. Lock the door if necessary; and if you are particularly sensitive to noise, use earplugs. Conduct your relaxation session in an upright chair. Don't lie down on a couch or bed: you are far too likely to fall asleep. If you are using autohypnosis or biofeedback, follow the instructions that came with your tapes or instruments. If you are doing it the hard way, the following sequence, quoted from my *Reincarnation Workbook,* may be of help:

Begin by regulating your breathing. Relaxation is a physical function. Your muscles use oxygen extracted from your bloodstream. Your bloodstream, in turn, extracts that oxygen from the air you breathe. By regulating your breathing, you increase the oxygen available in your blood, your muscles extract the optimum amount and are far happier to relax for you than they might otherwise be.

If you have studied yoga, you will know there are all sorts of complex breath-regulation techniques. But the one I want you to try is very simple. It is called 2/4 breathing.

What it comes down to is that you
1. Breathe in to the mental count of four . . .
2. Hold your breath in to the mental count of two . . .
3. Breathe out to the mental count of four . . .
4. Hold your breath out to the mental count of two.

It sounds simple and it is, although I should warn you there is a bit of a knack to getting it right. (You will know you have got it right, incidentally, when you begin doing it without thinking.)

The rate at which you should count varies from individual to individual. Start by synchronizing it with your heartbeat. If this doesn't work, play around until you hit on the rhythm that is most comfortable for you.

Get your breathing comfortable before you go on to the second part of the exercise.

Once you have established a comfortable rhythm of 2/4 breathing, let it run for about three minutes, then start the following relaxation sequence. (If you can hold the 2/4 rhythm while you do it, that's great, but chances are you will not be able to do so at first. In this latter case, just start your session with three minutes of 2/4 breathing, then go back to normal breathing while you carry out the main relaxation sequence, then take up 2/4 breathing again when you are nicely relaxed.)

Concentrate on your feet. Wiggle them about. Curl them to tense the muscles, then allow them to relax.

Concentrate next on your calf muscles. Tighten and relax them.

Concentrate on your thigh muscles. Tighten and relax them.

Concentrate on your buttock muscles. Tighten your buttocks and anus, then relax them.

Concentrate on your stomach muscles, a very common tension focus. Tighten then relax them.

Concentrate on your hands. Curl them into fists, then relax them.

Concentrate on your arms. Tighten them rigidly, then relax them.

Concentrate on your back. Tighten the muscles, then relax them.

Concentrate on your chest. Tighten the muscles, then relax them.

Concentrate on your shoulders, another very common tension focus. Hunch your shoulders to tighten the muscles, then relax them.

Concentrate on your neck. Tighten the muscles then relax them.

Concentrate on your face. Grit your teeth and contort your features to tense up the facial muscles then relax them.

Concentrate on your scalp. Frown to tighten the scalp muscles, then relax them.

Now tighten up every muscle in your body, holding your entire body momentarily rigid, then relax, letting go as completely as you are able. Do this final whole body sequence again, then again – three times in all. On the third time, take a really deep breath when you tense the muscles and sigh deeply aloud as you let the tension go.

You should be feeling nicely relaxed by now. If you abandoned your 2/4 breathing at the start of the relaxation sequence, pick it up again at this point.

Close your eyes and try to imagine your whole body getting heavier and heavier, as if it were turning to lead. You will find your visualization increases your level of relaxation still further.

Enjoy the sensation of relaxation for the remainder of your session. But stay vigilant. Should you find tension creeping in anywhere (and you certainly will in the early days) don't let it worry you. Just tighten up the tense muscles a little more, then relax them.

Use the technique regularly until you have trained yourself to relax totally any time you want to.

Complete physical relaxation is not the whole secret of etheric projection, but it is a large and important part of the whole secret. Another important part is a calm mind, again reported by some 79 per cent of respondents.

Many years ago, I worked as director of a clinic which taught relaxation among other self-improvement skills. A catch-phrase of the clinic was that *a totally relaxed body cannot harbour a destructive emotion.* In other words, when your body is completely relaxed, your mind must, by this definition, be calm. However accurate it might be, this catch-phrase was also a Catch-22. While your mind remains upset and disturbed, your chances of achieving total relaxation are minimal. Although complete relaxation and mental calm go hand in hand, they do so *all the way.* One does not suddenly appear from nowhere when the other is achieved.

You need to know plainly that to get the best out of the relaxation sequence I have just described, you must approach it in as worry-free a state as possible. There is some positive feedback involved in physical relaxation, so you may find some of your worries slipping away if you persevere, but you will progress far more quickly – and relax far more deeply – if you tackle your mental state head on. One of the best ways to do so is meditation.

A total of 27 per cent of respondents were actually engaged in meditation when projection occurred. This is not altogether surprising. In the East, projection is often experienced during yogic meditation – indeed often *expected*. Physical relaxation is generally a preliminary to meditation, the techniques of which tend to calm and still the mind. Even without further effort, the combination of these two factors is often enough to stimulate a spontaneous projection. As my favourite projector might have said, they facilitate the process of *letting go.*

But as you will quickly discover, the word *meditation* is like the phrase *astral projection* – it means different things to different people. There are, in fact, a whole series of meditational techniques, some better for our present purpose than others. When, for example, I was originally trained to meditate, I was taught how to follow specific chains of thought, how to manipulate imagery and how to avoid mind-wandering. It was a style of meditation well suited to a Western mind and one which developed an unusually high degree of concentration. Intensity of concentration does indeed block out worries, at least temporarily, but this is a long way from the tranquility generated by other methods.

Perhaps one of the most successful methods is the exercise of identification with an object or symbol – a technique called *contemplation* by the majority of Western religious orders, but a meditative technique none the less. The method is easily enough described. You begin with your symbol or object – a rose-bud, for example, might be a pleasant starting point – which you hold sufficiently close to enable you to examine it in minute detail. You attempt to familiarize yourself with the *totality* of the rose: the form, the scent, the weight, the feel, the colour. You meditate on the rose-bud's position in context, how it relates to other types of rose, other flowers, other plants, how it relates to the sun and the soil, where it stands within the universal whole.

All sorts of associations spin off from this exercise – far more than you would imagine until you actually try it. But these associations are unimportant in themselves; merely a way of getting mundane perceptions and linkages out of your system. Once you feel you have travelled that path sufficiently far, the core of the meditation presents itself. In this you reach out with your mind and attempt to imagine what it feels like to *be* a rose-bud. With practice, you will find eventually that close examination, or contemplation, of an object leads quickly to identification with it. The intermediate stage of categorization in relation to form, colour etc., no longer intrudes. In the final stage of the exercise, identification slips into a merging with the object of your contemplation. You *become* the rose-bud and, with any luck, experience a unity unavailable to mundane consciousness.

If you succeed in this adventure, I have no doubt you will achieve an unparalleled degree of tranquillity, not alone at the time, but for a long time afterwards as well. The problem is that contemplation to the level described is far from easy. On the evidence of religious mystics through the ages, you might have to work for years to get real results. Since you are only seeking to calm the mind (not achieve the ultimate experience of mystical unity) there must be an easier way. And there is.

If there is one fundamental connecting link between the various forms of meditation, it is the necessity to *still the mind*. This involves thinking of nothing at all, a process which, with practice, seems to lead automatically to a calmer form of general mentation. But thinking of nothing is a lot more difficult than it sounds. Even thinking of only one thing is a lot more difficult than it sounds. Try this simple test. Count mentally upwards from one, while *thinking of absolutely nothing else whatsoever*. As soon as an extraneous thought creeps in (like 'I'm going rather well here') stop counting. If you are observant and honest, you will be very lucky to get past 10 . . . unless you happen to be skilled in mind control.

Some people spend a great many years learning to still the mind, but there is a short-cut. This is the technique of *mantric* meditation. A good deal of superstitious nonsense has accumulated around the subject of mantras. But a mantra is simply a word or phrase which, when repeated, has an effect on the human mind. By this definition, a good many advertising slogans and jingles are mantras, as certainly was the salutation *Heil Hitler* in Germany during the Nazi period.

Advocates of Transcendental Meditation suggest the most potent mantras are personal, mysteriously attuned to the vibrations of the individuals who use them. For present purposes, you can make do with something far less elaborate – a circular mantra in daily use by millions throughout the Orient. This mantra goes *Aum mani padme hum*, and is associated with Buddhism. It usually translates 'Hail to the Jewel in the Lotus.' For those of you who worry about such things, the words are supposed to refer to the central core of enlightenment (the jewel) within the human soul. In point of fact, the *meaning* is of no importance whatsoever. What we are after is the *effect*, which might just as easily be obtained from the Islamic mantra *Hua allahu alazi lailaha illa Hua* ('He is God and there is no other God than He'), the Egyptian *A ka dua, Tuf ur biu, Bi aa chefu, Dudu ner af an nuteru* ('I adore the might of thy breath, supreme and terrible God, who makest the Gods and Death to tremble before Thee') or even *Three blind mice, see how they run. They all run after the farmer's wife. She cut off their tails with a carving knife. Did you ever see such a thing in your life as three blind mice. . .*

The common denominator between all these mantras is that they swallow their tails. You will see what I mean if you chant any one of them aloud. No sooner has the last word of the mantra been pronounced than you can begin it again from the beginning. Which is more or less what you should do to begin your mantric meditation practice. Sit comfortably where you will not be disturbed, go through your conscious relaxation as outlined earlier, then begin to chant the mantra *Aum mani padme hum*.

Try chanting it aloud at first. Make it sonorous and run the final *mmm* of *hum*

into the beginning of *aum*. The rhythm and pronunciation are as follows:
Aw-um mah-nee padmeh hummmmm um mah-nee padmeh hummm . . .

After you have listened to it aloud for a few cycles, lower the volume progressively until you 'withdraw' the sounds into your mind and continue pronouncing the mantric circle mentally. Experiment with speed until you find a rhythm which grips your attention so that extraneous thoughts are thrown out by the spinning mantra. The effect is very similar to those times when you get a tune into your head and can't get it out. The mantra spins and expands to fill your consciousness until there is no room for anything else. Even if you are aware of the meaning of the phrase you are using, that meaning is soon lost, in the same way that your mind blanks out the meaning of a word you repeat too often.

Once the spinning mantra is firmly established, it will continue with no conscious effort, leaving you free to relax more fully with an untroubled mind.

When you wish to return to your normal mode of consciousness, slow the spin rate of the mantra, then 'externalize' it by pronouncing it aloud a few times before stopping altogether.

6.

How to Make a Witch's Cradle

Profound physical relaxation, a calm mind, and a desire to travel, are factors present in a great many successful projections . . . and are enough, in themselves, to trigger projection in a small number of cases – perhaps 2 per cent to 3 per cent of those who persevere. If you are not among these latter lucky few, what other methods are open to you?

In sharp contrast to the majority, almost a quarter (23 %) of projectors polled indicated that they were *under emotional stress* at the time they left their bodies. This is a fascinating finding, for it takes us directly into the realm of shamanism, where initiatory rites are structured explicitly to *induce* stress. Closely associated with the stress factor is *unusual fatigue*, reported in 15 per cent of cases.

Many primitive communities (and several not so primitive) make use of the stress/fatigue approach in the form of rhythmic dancing to exhaustion or, like the Islamic dervishes, whirling to produce extreme disorientation. Projections are not uncommon among participants of such ceremonies and if you have the stamina for it, you can try your hand at duplicating this methodology.

What anthropologists call 'cultural factors' are important – in this context the beliefs and expectations of the ceremonial participants. Stress and fatigue *per se* are not (usually) enough, otherwise every disco would be awash with startled projectors. The essential catalyst seems to be *expectation*. If you *expect* to project at a certain point in the ceremony – and if that point coincides with a moment of high stress and unusual fatigue – then your chances of projection are appreciably heightened. Other equally unlikely methods exist, a fact to which Jack London's last published novel, *The Star Rover*, bears eloquent testimony. The fictional hero of the book was based on an actual personage, an American convict named Ed Morrell.

Morrell was a difficult prisoner and the Arizona State Penitentiary had a barbarous policy towards difficult prisoners. They were strapped into two strait-jackets, which were then soaked in water. As the jackets dried, they shrank, crushing the unfortunate within – a form of legalized torture. Inevitably, the shrinking strait-jackets were applied to Morell, who found himself unable to breathe, with lights dancing before his eyes. But then something very unexpected happened – he found himself free, *outside* the prison. It was, of course, an etheric projection. His physical body remained uncomfortably bound . . . and apparently asleep.

Morrell frequently fell foul of the prison authorities, but each time the strait-jacket punishment was applied, his etheric body walked free. They were valid projections. He was able to bring back information on the world outside the penitentiary. George W.P. Hunt, the Governor of Arizona, testified to the fact that Morrell was witness to events which took place while his body remained in its cell.

Morrell was not a natural projector. Unless subject to the cruel and unusual punishment of the strait-jackets, he was never able to leave his body.

Colin Wilson, who mentions the case in his book *Mysteries*, suggests it was pain which caused Morrell to project – and certainly this is likely to have been a factor: some 6 per cent of polled projectors mentioned severe pain as a pre-existent condition to their experience. But pain may not have been the only factor. Indeed, I suspect a number of factors may have interlinked.

If you are trapped into a brace of shrinking strait-jackets, one thing that precedes even the pain is immobility. And as the jackets shrink, the degree of immobility increases. When the pain eventually begins, physical immobility is underscored by a sort of mental immobility. Pain, like hanging, concentrates the mind wonderfully. If you have a toothache, it is all you can think about. If you are being squeezed by a shrinking strait-jacket, the pain quickly grows to fill your entire horizon. Eventually your system goes on overload. You cease to react to stimulus or, more correctly, you cease to react to stimulus other than the overriding pain. The bottom line, oddly enough, is not a million miles away from sensory deprivation.

Sensory deprivation experiments have been popular for some years now, since their findings are relevant to things like space flight and submarine warfare. Typically, volunteers are submerged in light-proof tanks, sometimes floating in lukewarm water, often with padded gloves and clothing. The idea is to cut down external sensory input to a point as close to zero as possible. In such situations, the average volunteer will spend the first eight to ten hours catching up on sleep, a few more hours amusing him/herself with recitations and song, and the rest of the experiment hallucinating. At least, the military scientists who have conducted the majority of these experiments *assume* their subjects have been hallucinating. Anyone with experience of projection might not be quite so sure, for among the records of *real* hallucinations (like the one in which a small man, nude except for a tin hat, rowed a galvanized metal bath across the subject's field of vision) are a number which read far more like astral plane projections and a few which suggest etheric out-of-body experiences.

Official experiments in sensory deprivation are high-technology affairs. The tanks are linked up to systems not at all unlike the life-supports found in spacecraft. Instruments measure the subject's respiration, heart rate, blood pressure, mobility and EEG traces. Communication links are there for visual observation and, in the other direction, to allow the subject to terminate the experiment should things get out of hand. In underwater experiments, a reliable air supply is of obvious importance. And so on. But similar results may be obtained by distinctly low-tech means. Centuries ago, Craft occultists perfected a sensory deprivation aid to etheric (and astral plane) projection known as the *witch's cradle*.

You can construct a witch's cradle by finding, or making, a sack large enough to hold you while you are standing upright and strong enough to support you if it was lifted while you were inside. Since you *will* be inside when the cradle is in use, it is as well to stress that plastic or any other air-tight material should be avoided because of the danger of suffocation. Coarse, strong, loose-weave sacking is probably the most ideal, close to the original Craft design and cheap. The neck of the sack should be fastenable by a draw-string and the whole thing arranged so that it may be suspended safely with a subject inside.

To use the cradle, you will need a reliable colleague, a high beam or a stout tree and a free night. Purists might add thick gloves, ear-plugs and a blindfold, although in practice these are seldom necessary. If you are experimenting out of doors in winter (or even in most British summers) make sure you are wearing warm, comfortable clothing.

For the site of your experiment you need somewhere isolated (hence quiet) where the cradle can be suspended a foot or so off the ground. Historically, Craft users selected a strong-branched tree in some secluded spot, but it is often easier, always more comfortable, and just as effective to stay indoors so long as your location is guaranteed free from disturbance and noise.

You need to set aside a full night – at least – for your experiment. Have your colleague help you into the sack, which is then suspended while you remain in an upright, standing position. Do nothing more for a few minutes while you check to ensure there is a good air supply within the sack. Then, assuming everything is all right, have your colleague spin and swing you, sack and all, first one way then another, until you are thoroughly disorientated. You are then left to your own devices. Left, that is, free from interference, but certainly not alone. Your colleague should – indeed *must* – remain close throughout the experiment in order to terminate it at once should any major problem arise. He/she should remain quiet throughout, until such time as you signal the end of the session.

From your own viewpoint, inside the sack, you will begin the experiment disorientated to the point where you have no sense of cardinal direction; and may eventually lose the ability to discriminate between down and up. There is some suggestion that you should remain standing for as long as possible, but while this certainly introduces the fatigue factor discussed earlier, it does not really seem to make a great deal of difference to overall results. So stand, squat or lie within the sack and await developments.

The sack is not, of course, lightproof, nor should it be since any attempt to make it so will probably render it airtight as well: a situation guaranteed to ensure any out-of-body experience you achieve is permanent. This is why the experiment is carried out at night, or in a lightless room. The initial disorientation, the darkness, the quiet and the obvious difficulties in obtaining much differentiated tactile stimulation inside a suspended sack, all add up to a high degree of sensory deprivation. As with many shamanistic techniques – a category to which this one certainly belongs – mindset and expectation are important. In other words, bear in mind the reason you got yourself into such a peculiar situation. Expect nothing (except possibly some interesting panic feelings) for the first half of the night. If you do achieve a projection, it will almost certainly happen towards the latter end of the experiment.

The witch's cradle is one of the more lonely and uncomfortable methods of stimulating etheric projection. If you carry it through – with or without results – you might like to reward yourself by attempting another approach which is neither lonely nor uncomfortable: sexual orgasm. Among the polled projectors, orgasm featured as a pre-existent condition in only 3 per cent of cases, but I suspect the statistics. Even in the era of permissiveness, people are notoriously reticent about discussing their sex lives, so that orgasm may have been a factor in far more cases than the figures indicate. Certainly my own experience clearly suggests a particular type of sexual experience can very easily trigger a projection, although the end result seems to be a little more common among women than men.

But the emphasis here must be placed on those words *particular type.* There is no direct causal connection between simple orgasm and etheric projection, otherwise out-of-body experiences would be too commonplace to require an *Astral Projection Workbook.* Orgasm, of course, involves the simultaneous firing of a great many neuron synapses. In this respect, the nearest thing to it is a sneeze. Interestingly, a great many people still say 'Bless you' when someone sneezes, a throwback to an old belief that the soul momentarily leaves the body. (The blessing ensures no invading entity will take it over before the rightful owner returns.)

Male orgasm is typically a genital affair. Women, by contrast, are often slower to reach climax, but tend to experience more of a whole-body involvement when they get there. The projective experience, for both men and women arises most often in cases of intense whole-body (or, more properly, whole-body/mind) involvement. One of the first steps towards bringing this about is temporary celibacy. The keyword, you will be relieved to hear, is *temporary.* Celibacy is not, in this instance, the road to spiritual enlightenment, but simply a means of increasing frustration and building up sexual tensions. There is no need, for example, to avoid sexual stimulation – rather the reverse. The greater the level of advance arousal, the more chance there is of holistic involvement at the point of tension discharge (orgasm).

In the experiment itself – if experiment is an appropriate word in the circumstances – all efforts should be directed towards the pleasant task of achieving maximum arousal and maintaining it as long as possible. This is a tightrope act, of course, but with care, patience and, above all, self-control, it is possible to hold on the edge of orgasm for very long periods – up to eight hours or more.

Men in particular are prone to go over the edge too quickly in this sort of situation, but breath control (i.e. deep, rhythmic breathing) or firm pressure on the base of the penis will usually enable a retreat from the brink. This degree of control is generally far more important for a man than a woman since, with males, it is the first orgasm following a lengthy period of celibacy and arousal which is the most intense. For women capable of multiple orgasm, however, the reverse appears to be the case with *increasing* intensity experienced as one orgasm follows another. (Up to a point, that is. Many women who enjoy multiple orgasm find that exhaustion fairly quickly overcomes arousal, even among the youngest and fittest.)

Having created and held a situation of maximum arousal, you should aim for the old ideal of *simultaneous* orgasm by both partners. It is not absolutely crucial to projection, but it does seem to increase the probability of success. What *is* important is a total *letting go* at the point when orgasm finally arrives. Unless you have sexual problems – in which case you would obviously be well-advised to try a different projection method altogether – the time and energy you have invested into preparation will normally make this easy, even instinctive.

The subjective experience of orgasmic projection is extremely pleasant, if a little uncontrollable. For both men and women, the type of orgasm which does the trick triggers in the genital area, but rolls along the entire body in an upwards sweeping sensation which carries consciousness – and, I presume, the second body – out through the top of the head.

Like some other methods mentioned, orgasmic projection can result in either etheric or astral plane experiences. Where the result is etheric projection, you will typically find yourself out of the body and floating a distance above it – sometimes a considerable distance above it. This a characteristic orgasmic projection shares with spontaneous projection following an accident and many projections which involve general anaesthesia.

Since, by definition, you are seldom alone while using this method, it is one of the few approaches in which the likelihood arises of finding yourself out of the body *with a friend*. This has never happened to me in an etheric projection (although I have found it fairly commonplace in astral plane experiments) but I understand that your partner's etheric body is perfectly visible, *and tangible* to you in the projected state. This is particularly interesting since, as we have already noted, physical matter is *intangible* while you are in the projected state.

It is possible, although not particularly easy, for one out-of-body partner to help the other to achieve projection. Contrary to some of the more popular esoteric myths, I have found little evidence to suggest that a projected friend can actually pull your etheric body out of the physical body if the two are fully integrated. But projection is seldom as clear cut as 'all in' or 'all out.' Situations frequently arise where you will project only partially, like Monroe's experience when he was lying with one projected arm pushed through the floor, or begin to come out, but slip back in again before achieving total projection. In situations of this sort, a projected partner can sometimes help by gently pulling. But he/she really should be very gentle since any overt interference with your etheric body triggers fear and even panic reactions very easily; and these, of course, act to force the etheric back into the physical body. Assisted projections, if they are managed at all, work best when the two people involved enjoy deep bonds of emotional intimacy and trust.

7.

Scientific Projection

If Robert Monroe or Sylvan Muldoon ever climbed into a witch's cradle or cultivated intense whole-body orgasms in order to project, they never wrote about it. Each evolved his own techniques, largely based on personal experience. Hardly surprisingly, certain aspects of their techniques overlap not only with each other, but with aspects of the methods already examined.

Driven by a desire to discover more about his peculiar talent, Monroe founded the Monroe Institute of Applied Sciences. Its first laboratory had a research wing which contained an instrument room, three isolation booths and a briefing room. Each booth contained a heated water-bed and was environmentally controlled in terms of air supply, acoustics and temperature. Subjects could be monitored for EEG readings, pulse rate, EMG (muscle tone) and galvanic skin response.

As a qualified engineer with a career background in broadcasting, Monroe was led towards the use of sound as an aid to out-of-body experience. In 1975, his Institute received a patent for a process called Frequency Following Response (FFR), based on the intriguing discovery that certain sound patterns, fed into a subject's ear, produced a similar brainwave pattern. The discovery enabled the use of sound as an aid to creating and maintaining those states most conducive to projection. One such state was labelled Focus 10, in which all the body's physiological signs are those of sleep, but EEG monitors show an overlay of waking brainwave patterns.

Sometimes the sound-triggered Focus 10 state is all that is needed to facilitate a projection. During one early experiment, a Kansas psychiatrist used Monroe's patented sound signal on four subjects without giving them any indication what results might be expected. One of the four quickly opted out of the experiment. He had, he said, found himself bouncing against the ceiling of the room while looking down on his physical body.

The FFR process was followed by another discovery which was, if anything, even more intriguing. Monroe called this process Hemi-Sync. Hemi-Sync arose out of research into the function of specific brain structures, which itself developed from a surgical procedure aimed at the control of epilepsy. For a long time it has been known that the brain is divided into twin hemispheres, linked by a relatively narrow band of connecting tissue called the *corpus callosum*.

Epilepsy involves periodic uncontrolled electrical discharges within the brain – a sort of miniature storm – which typically begins at a specific site, but quickly spreads to give the symptoms of *grand mal* or full-blown epileptic fit.

In the early 1960s, it became fashionable to treat severely epileptic patients by severing the connecting tissue between the two brain hemispheres. The theory was that if the disease could not be cured, it might at least be confined to a single hemisphere and the symptoms consequently reduced. The procedure worked. A marked degree of relief was obtained. Furthermore, the patients appeared none the worse for having the two halves of their brain cut adrift. It seemed, for a time, that humanity was equipped with not one brain but two – that one half acted as a sort of 'spare' for the other.

But further research with split-brain patients showed this was not, in fact, the case. Each of the brain's hemispheres actually specializes. In about 90 per cent of the population, the left hemisphere controls motor movement in the right side of the body and deals with 'logical' functions like language, writing, arithmetical calculation etc. The right hemisphere controls the left side of the body and is the seat of 'creative' function like drawing, perception of spatial relationships, imagination and so on.

Monroe's Hemi-Sync was actually an ingenious application of the Frequency Following Response. It used sound patterns fed through separate channels into each of the two ears to produce a *synchronized* response in each brain hemisphere. In other words, the right and left brains were persuaded to generate identical wave forms at the same time.

Aided by this whole array of tools and techniques, Monroe was able to report (In *Far Journeys* which was published in Britain in 1986) that his Institute had processed more than 3,000 subjects through a 'Gateway Program' designed to help them develop awareness of differing states of consciousness . . . including the out-of-body experience. This is all very well if you can get to Monroe's Institute – or raise the substantial funds necessary for the high-tech approach, but for most of us what is needed is a train-at-home technology, a do-it-yourself Gateway Program which would enable us to obtain similar results in return for a larger investment of effort. To his credit, Monroe has developed just such a programme, which he described in great detail in his first book *Journeys Out Of The Body*.

Like Sylvan Muldoon, Monroe believes it likely that most – indeed probably all – of us leave our bodies unconsciously during sleep. Despite this, his investigations suggest the one great obstacle to etheric projection is something he has called the Fear Barrier. Most of us, it seems, are nervous of leaving our physical bodies. It is a blind, unreasoning fear which, if projection seems imminent, can quickly turn to terror, even panic. Unconscious projections (like my own midnight walks when I was aware of leaving the body, but had no idea how I managed it) seem to leap-frog this barrier, but any attempt to develop a fully conscious projection technique runs into it full tilt.

There is no easy way around this. Monroe himself analysed the Barrier into three component parts – fear of dying, fear of not being able to return to the physical body and fear of the unknown. Reading books such as this one must help a little. They can provide some reassurance that projection will not kill you, and returning to your body is as easy as wiggling your big toe. And they can tell you in detail what to expect during and after a projection. But reading about space flight is not the same as travelling to the moon and while preparation can minimize the Fear Barrier, you may as well accept your first few attempts at projection will be frightening experiences. And the more successful they are, the more frightening they are likely to be.

The only way through the Fear Barrier is determination. The only way to flatten it is familiarity and experience. Once you have successfully projected a few times, you *know* what to expect. You *know* it will not kill you. And you *know* you can get back into your body any time you wish. Gradually the fear subsides. Eventually it will disappear altogether. But for your first attempts, recognize that you are going to be afraid, take your courage in boths hands and *persevere*.

The first stage of Monroe's technique is relaxation. If you are still not entirely proficient with the relaxation techniques already given, you might like to try a new one, which Monroe calls the *borderland sleep state*. This technique is straightforward, but tricky. When you go to bed tonight and begin to drift into sleep, fix your mental attention on a particular thought and hold it.

Almost certainly you will not be able to hold it for very long the first few times: you will simply fall asleep as usual. But if you practise diligently, you will find you are gradually able to extend the period in which you balance between waking and sleeping states. Monroe warns that your first attempts at this exercise can make you nervous – the mind seems to resent any interference with its normal functioning. If this happens, break the relaxation, get up and walk around, then come back to bed and try again. If the nervousness persists, abandon your experiment and try again another night.

Monroe has coined the term *Condition A* to describe the ability to lie indefinitely between sleep and waking, eyes closed and the mind focused on a single though or picture. When you have achieved it, you are ready to pass on to *Condition B*.

Condition B is actually very similar to Condition A, except that you no longer concentrate on an anchor thought. Instead you simply lie there staring with closed eyes at the blackness ahead of you. There is a possibility of visual hallucinations at this stage, sometimes quite vivid. These appear to be related to your activities prior to going to bed. Thus you might experience a rerun of a tennis tournament you watched on TV or, as I have managed quite frequently, see the pages of a bedtime novel you were reading. You can assume expertise in Condition B when any nervousness and hallucinations have faded away and you are able to hold the state as long as you wish, staring into darkness.

Condition C, the stage that follows, is achieved by carefully graded practice. You allow yourself to drift a little deeper into sleep by carefully controlled stages – or rather, you let your *body* drift a little deeper into sleep by carefully controlled stages. This is difficult to get right, but once again practice will allow you to succeed. Each successive stage is marked by the shut-down of a particular sense. Touch will normally go first and you will find you are no longer aware of tactile sensations. Smell and taste go next, then auditory input and finally vision.

As you will have noticed, the state you have now reached is similar, possibly even identical, to the Focus 10 state generated by Monroe's high-tech techniques. In other words, your body falls asleep while your mind remains awake. You will also have noted the links with the sensory deprivation experiments mentioned earlier. Sensory input has been cut off, but by a training process rather than being imposed from the outside by some device like the witch's cradle. Having achieved Condition C through regular bedtime practice, you need to gain the ability to pass into the state at any time – not merely when you are tired and ready for sleep. One good tip is to start practising immediately after waking up, before getting out of bed, since the body is usually very relaxed at this time.

The Focus 10 body-asleep/mind-awake state can, of course, be achieved by other means. Once you know what you are looking for, hypnosis or autohypnosis will do the trick, as will deep progressive relaxation and some forms of meditation. But Focus 10 is only a part of the conscious projection process. The whole technique, which will carry you all the way through to an out-of-body experience, is as follows:

Step One
Find a room where you will not be disturbed. Set yourself no deadline and try to ensure you have nothing else to do except the experiment. Darken the room, but not completely – you need to retain a visual reference with your eyes open, but ensure no light filters through your eyelids when they are closed. Lie down in a comfortable position with your head towards magnetic north and your body along the north/south axis. (Some people have long suspected they slept better when their bed was oriented north/south. Whatever about this, Monroe's research indicated there was a small statistical bias towards successful projection in this position.)

Step 2
Enter the Focus 10 state – body asleep/mind awake – using any method you have previously found to work for you. When the state is achieved, mentally repeat half a dozen times that you will consciously perceive and remember all that happens to you during the experiment. Begin to breathe regularly through your half open mouth.

Step 3
Stare through the blackness (with your eyes closed) to a point about a foot in front of your forehead. Push your concentration three feet away, then six feet. Hold your gaze focused on this point six feet in front of your forehead until you have it firmly and clearly established. Once it is firmly established, swing the point of focus backwards in a 90° arc so that you end up with your attention focused on a point above (behind) the top of your head, six feet distant on a line running along your body axis.

As you focus on this point, you will be aware of vibrations. The sensation is subtle, very peculiar, but quite distinctive as if something was vibrating on the spot and you were sensing it on the edge of your perception. Mentally reach out and *draw the vibrations into your body*. Once you have located and drawn in the vibrations a few times over a series of experiments, you will typically find you have only to achieve Focus 10 and think of the vibrations to start them buzzing in your body, thus short-cutting the process a little.

Step 4
Give yourself time to allow any fear reaction to die down. The vibrations are, of course, the same vibrations Monroe himself felt when he first began to project spontaneously. They were so bizarre, so alien to his normal experience, that he was convinced he was ill and sought medical help. Even with the information in this workbook under your belt, it is still very difficult to keep a cool head when the vibrations start. To make matters worse, should you try to struggle at this point, you will find your body paralysed. You *can* break paralysis if you try really hard, but it involves a substantial effort of will and, of course, terminates an experiment you have worked very hard to set up.

If you avoid panic, work on your fear and simply observe the vibrations, they will die down of their own accord after approximately five minutes – although it can *seem* substantially longer the first time you are waiting for it to happen.

Step 5
When you have control of your fear reactions, the time comes to take control of the vibrations. Call them up again if necessary, then using your mind, form them into a ring at your head. When you have succeeded in doing this, push them down your body to your feet. After you have practised controlling the vibrations in this way, start them sweeping down your body in a rhythmic wave, from head to feet then back again. Continue to do so until they fade.

You can assume expertise in this step when you are able to call up the vibrations instantly and keep them coursing along your body without pause until they fade.

Step Six
The natural 'raw' vibrations are those which Monroe felt during his earliest experiences, a sensation which can seem very similar at times to shaking from malaria, or travelling too fast in an old car with unbalanced wheels. Your next step is to refine them. You can do this by causing them to pulse as you send them along your body. The effect shows only slowly, but eventually you will find the vibrations grow smoother. It is as if they have increased their rate of frequency, a process which continues to build until, like high frequency sound, you are no longer really aware of them at all. You may notice a pleasant tingling warmth in your body, however.

Step Seven
By this stage of the technique, it is important to control your thoughts and

desires, for you are very close indeed to projection and it is entirely possible for an errant visualization to send you out and to a destination where you really do not want to go.

In order to achieve smooth dissociation of the etheric body, practise reaching for something by stretching your arm. If all goes well, you will extend your etheric arm out of your physical body, something which may be tested by pushing it into or through a solid object. Once you have succeeded, withdraw the projected arm back into the physical body, decrease the vibrations, move your body and open your eyes.

Experiment with these partial projections until you are entirely comfortable with them.

Step Eight

Having again achieved the high-frequency vibrationary state, imagine yourself growing lighter and floating upwards. You will find after a few attempts that this is exactly what you will do . . . leaving your physical body behind. Alternatively, some people find it easier to *roll* out of the physical – which is what I found myself doing during some of my own spontaneous projections.

Whichever technique you use, practise returning to the physical and realigning. If you have any problems, think of moving a physical limb or wiggling the big toe and you will be 'clicked' back in. When you are happy with your ability to enter and leave the body at will, try moving a little further away. Your full-scale etheric projections have begun.*

*Probably. Monroe has more recently gone on record with the opinion that this method is unreliable since it takes no account of important factors discovered later. My own experience has been that no single method is guaranteed to work for everybody, but this one gets results for a lot of people and is well worth a try if you are prepared to invest the necessary effort.

8.

Preparing to Project

Sylvan Muldoon was the product of a different age from that of Robert A. Monroe and talked a different language when it came to creating projection techniques. Not for him such space age expressions as Focus 10 and Gateway Program. Like Monroe, he felt there were a variety of factors involved in projection, but expressed them in terms like desire, need and habit.

Desire might be intense or suppressed, but not sexual, since he believed a state of (unsatisfied) arousal tended to lock the etheric into the physical. Need was defined as a physical priority. Muldoon listed hunger, thirst and 'lack of cosmic energy.' I would tend to add the necessity of emptying a full bladder. Habit might be some long-standing ritual or simply a routine way of doing things.

None of these factors induce projection *in themselves,* but Muldoon felt that if they arose while the physical body was *incapacitated* they had a distinct tendency to pull out the etheric. His theory was that the unconscious mind, desperate to satisfy the need or desire – or simply driven by habit – would make a symbolic gesture to do so. Since illness left him physically incapacitated for long periods, it is likely that he experienced the fruits of this theory on a great many occasions, without particular effort. For those less fortunate, however, he developed a number of techniques based on his insights.

First, he tackled the problem of *inducing incapacity.* To do this, he advocated a voluntary slackening of the pulse – something which, he maintained, also triggered concentration and relaxation. You lie on your back (or right side) hands by your sides, then take a deep breath forcing it down to the pit of your stomach, so that the abdomen bulges outwards. Exhale completely, using your stomach muscles to empty the lungs totally.

Repeat this process eight times.

Close your eyes and picture yourself in your mind. Starting at the top of your head, picture your scalp, then tense and relax the muscles which control it. Move down to your jaw, picture it, tense and relax it. Next think of your neck, tense and relax it a few times. Continue in sequence to your upper arms, your lower arms, your hands. Then beginning at the base of the neck, go down the entire body tensing and relaxing each part until you reach your toes.

This is, of course, very similar to the conscious relaxation exercise given earlier, but Muldoon is aiming for more than simple relaxation.

Think next of your heart (in a relaxed, unworried manner) and try to sense its beat. Keep trying until you can hear and feel the heartbeat distinctly.

Your next step is to feel and hear the pulse in any part of the body you select, simply by concentrating on the part. This is not actually nearly so difficult as you might imagine, but like most of these techniques, it does require practice. Look for a pulse, in sequence, in your chest, your neck, your cheeks, the top of your head, back down to cheeks, neck, chest, stomach, abdomen, both thighs, calves and feet. Come back up to the calves again, then concentrate on the right thigh to prove to yourself how selective you can be in sensing the pulse. Muldoon remarks that if you concentrate on the *medulla oblongata* (back of the head) region, the pulse sensation there is almost identical to the pulse felt where the 'silver cord' joins the etheric body when you are projected.

Once you have succeeded in clearly sensing the pulse at will anywhere in your body, return your concentration to the heart region (where, obviously, you will feel the pulse as clearly as anywhere else.) Will a steady, smooth rhythm, mentally echoing the beat. Then, when you have synchronized your mental beat with the pulse in the chest, slow the mental beat slightly and will the heart to follow suit.

This is, I suppose, a good time to repeat Muldoon's own warning that the exercise – and indeed etheric projection as a whole – should be left severely alone if you suffer from any sort of heart condition. He is of the opinion that all projections involve a considerable drop in heart rate and consequently might place too much strain on an already weakened organ. It is an area about which you must make up your own mind. In my experience *not* all projections involve a lowered heartbeat, although some certainly do. Furthermore, it would appear to me that a slowed heart rate would take some strain off that important organ, not put more on. As against that, there is a very small chance in interfering with the workings of *any* automatic body process that you may have trouble letting it revert to normal. This seldom happens and I have yet to find any case where it led to permanent damage, but it can certainly be very frightening and uncomfortable while it lasts.

How far you should attempt to slow your heart beat is a matter for your own judgement; although I hope I do not have to tell you that you should avoid stopping it altogether. What you are looking for is a marked degree of physical relaxation, torpor or incapacity. In Muldoon's own case, this was achieved at 42 beats per minute, but varies widely according to the individual. My stepson, who has made a fetish of fitness, has a resting heart rate of 42 beats per minute with no noticeable torpor unless there is work to be done.

Muldoon linked physical incapacity with sleep before he felt there was any real certainty of success in a projection – a point we will get back to in a lot more detail later. He also felt it necessary that you develop a *consciousness of self*, an intriguing notion which led to this unusual exercise:

Step 1
Set up a chair before a full-length mirror. Sit in the chair, relax and study

yourself in the mirror not as if you were looking at a reflection, but rather as if you were actually seeing yourself from the outside. Try to imagine that is the *real* you in the mirror.

Step 2
Scrutinize yourself in detail trying to discover things about yourself that you never noticed before. Imagine you are meeting yourself for the first time . . . and are required to write such a detailed description of this strange personage that it could be used to identify you in a Court of Law. Don't be tempted to hurry this step – take as much time as you need.

Step 3
Stand up, directly in front of the mirror, and stare directly into your reflected eyes. Hold your own eyes until you begin to feel unsteady and start to sway.

Step 4
Sit down again and once more lock your gaze on your reflected eyes. Begin to repeat your own name over and over, aloud, in a monotone. This step creates a measure of confusion which you should reinforce by strongly imagining that your real self is that reflection in the mirror; that, in other words, the essential you is *out there*.

The exercise is one of preparation, not projection and however confused you become at Step 4, Muldoon does not suggest this will lead to an out-of-body experience. Rather he believes the whole sequence implants in your unconscious the strong suggestion that you are out there some distance from your body and the unconscious will consequently aid you to project more effectively when you apply the other techniques.

Induction of stresses, like habit and thirst, are common sense procedures. Virtually any habit or routine may be built up and the body then incapacitated so that the habit cannot be followed. Something like thirst is induced by the simple expedient of denying yourself fluids, although Muldoon adds the interesting psychological pressure of ensuring a drink is visibly and readily available when you do so. Once again, when the physical body is incapacitated, the desperate subconscious will send the etheric out to fetch the water.*

All these techniques were linked by Muldoon to sleep. He was convinced the etheric moved slightly out of coincidence with the physical during sleep in order to absorb the cosmic energy the Hindus call *prana* and the Chinese call *ch'i*. He also believed that almost everyone experienced much fuller projections during sleep, but these were uncontrolled and unconscious, although sometimes remembered in a distorted form as dreams. Dreams of flying, falling, or associated activities like travelling in a lift, levitation or swimming he believed to be particularly significant. The belief is shared by Monroe, who went on record with this interesting statement:

*If the body is *not* sufficiently incapacitated, these techniques will tend to induce sleep-walking.

'We generally recognize that the flying dream, with or without an aircraft, is a rationalization of an OBE which is unacceptable to the belief system of the conscious mind. Later data suggests that the dream of getting out of your car and performing some act falls into a similar category. Have you ever dreamed that you forgot where you parked your car! Also, the falling dream often becomes re-entry into the physical when practised in slow motion.'

This agreement between experts is not altogether surprising, for careful analysis of Muldoon's central technique compared with that of Monroe, clearly indicates they are both approaching the same methodology from different angles. Monroe considered a prerequisite of projection was to achieve a state in which the mind was awake and the body asleep. Muldoon believed essentially that projections occurred while *both* mind and body were asleep, the trick being to wake up while it was happening.

Although less interesting than Monroe's method in some respects, this latter approach has its advantages. Using it, you seldom experience the vibrations mentioned by Monroe; and you will often leap-frog the Fear Barrier altogether. Muldoon further believed that it was possible to ensure a sleeping projection actually took place. The method he used was ingenious – dream control. His description of the technique carries echoes of Monroe's instructions for achieving Focus 10.

Step 1
Set aside several weeks in which you should undertake to observe yourself during the process of falling asleep. Concentrate your thoughts and try to become aware of your own consciousness growing dim as you slip into sleep. Work to retain the realization that you are awake and observing, even as wakefulness deserts you.

Step 2
When you have established the knack of holding onto consciousness so that you remain alert and in control well into the hypnogogic period, you must use this period to *construct a dream*.

There are two vital points to remember while creating your dream: a) It must permit you to take an *active* role and b) The action must correspond to the movement experienced in a projection.

Point a) is straightforward enough, but point b) requires a little explanation. In a projection, your etheric body will normally move upwards and outwards from your physical body. Dream actions which would correspond to this might be taking off in an aeroplane, flying a balloon, launching a hang-glider, climbing a ladder or simply going up in a lift. This little list is not meant to be definitive. You can use any of these ideas, or find your own dream analogy, so long as you select something you *enjoy doing*. I suffer from a fear of flying, so taking off in an aircraft would be useless for me. But since I have no claustrophobia, I quite enjoy travelling in a lift.

Step 3

Start the dream drama in motion *before* you fall asleep. Since by this stage you will be practised in retaining consciousness throughout the hypnogogic (falling asleep) period you can imagine the dream beginning. You might, for example, imagine yourself lying on the floor of a lift and tell yourself that as you enter sleep, the lift is going to move upwards, carrying you pleasantly and smoothly to an upper floor. Direct the dream so that you are indeed carried up, get out on the top floor and explore, then return to the lift and descend to where you began.

Step 4

Use the same dream night after night. This is particularly important since it is a signal to your unconscious, the part of you that actually triggers the projection. Experimenting with different dreams each night only confuses the picture and ensures no clear signal gets through.

In the quoted example, you can expect to project as you leave the elevator on the top floor and interiorize as you return having looked around a bit. You can also expect to *remember* the dream.

Although Muldoon insists a properly constructed dream will *always* project the phantom, you are going to have to take his word for it until you learn how to wake up while in the projected state. Sometimes, of course, this will happen spontaneously, but if you prefer not to trust to luck, Muldoon gives two wake-up methods. One of these, oddly enough, is to use an alarm clock (or some similar sound source).

Sounds will wake you up just as efficiently when you have projected as they will while you are asleep in your physical body. But there are problems. The first is that a frightening or startling noise will tend to jerk you back into the physical body, so select a soft, persistent tone in preference to a clanging alarm. The second is that *any* sound, however mellow, will take you back into the physical body if your phantom happens to be too close to the body when it occurs.

These problems tend to make the alarm clock approach unreliable. Fortunately, the alternative seems to have no drawbacks at all. This is to build a wake-up suggestion into your constructed dream.

The method requires work. First, you need to examine the dream you have constructed and decide at what point it will trigger an actual projection. Next, you have to decide at what stage in the dream your (unconscious) etheric body will be sufficiently far away from the physical body for you to wake up without shocking yourself back. Finally, you will need to examine your room and try to decide *where* your etheric body is likely to wake up – the area of your room, in other words, which equates with the wake-up point in your dreams.

It is important to be clear about the last of those steps. As you dream your special dream, (about going up in the lift, for example) your etheric body will separate from the physical. You will not be aware of this; only of the dream. But each element of the dream coincides with some action of your sleep-walking etheric body. The dream becomes a symbolic expression of what you are doing in the projected state. What you are now trying to do is decide just what those actions are likely to be.

This is probably a little easier than it sounds since – to continue with the example of the lift – you might decide that your moment of separation must come as you leave the lift on the top floor and if you then enter a dream room similar in size, and possibly in furnishings, to your own, it is a reasonably safe assumption that your dream location will correspond more or less with the physical location of your phantom.

Once you have found the physical location of your chosen wake-up point – or as close and reasonable an approximation as you can manage – you should follow the route of your projection in your physical body. When you reach the spot where you have decided to wake up, tell yourself confidently that this is exactly what you will do. Reinforce the suggestion by visualizing yourself remembering to awaken at the relevant point of the constructed dream.

Dream control is a little more pleasant, a little less frightening than Monroe's Focus 10 approach, but no less difficult. And equipment like the witch's cradle does not appeal to everyone. Furthermore, as we have already noted, many of the techniques already examined are essentially based on the same fundamental approach: you somehow keep your mind alert and active while persuading your body to fall into a state of passivity, incapacity or sleep.

The question naturally arises: is there another way? Not simply a different variation on what Monroe calls Focus 10, but something based on a totally different *principle*. The answer to this question is yes; and the method is far from new.

9.

The Body of Light

The day you joined the Golden Dawn, that magical Victorian Order which has so profoundly influenced modern occult thought, you were sworn to secrecy with these disturbing words:

> If I break this, my Magical Obligation, I submit myself, by my own consent, to a Stream of Power, set in motion by the Divine Guardians of this Order, Who live in the Light of their Perfect Justice, and before Whom my Soul now stands. They journey as upon the Winds. They strike where no man strikes. They slay where no man slays. And as I bow my neck under the Sword of the Hiereus, so do I commit myself unto their Hands for vengeance or reward.

One of the secrets you were sworn to conceal was something called the Body of Light technique. It was a method of triggering an out-of-body experience. Like everything else, the Body of Light technique requires practice, but you are not asked to hold yourself balanced in a hypnogogic state or take control of your dreams. All you are asked to do is use your imagination.

Begin by finding a comfortable chair in a room where you will not be disturbed. Then relax, using any method you find works for you. Deep, trance-like relaxation is definitely *not* required. Simply let go of your worries and muscular tensions so you can concentrate on the job at hand. Now imagine you are no longer seated in your chair, but standing in the room at a spot about six feet away. Try to visualize yourself standing there as clearly as you can. Make a real effort to paint in *detail*. Don't just settle for a vague, imaginary shape. Try to 'see' what you are wearing. Imagine the scuff marks on your shoes. Count the buttons on your jacket. Note the way your hair falls over one eye. Examine the expression on your face. Visualize in colour and in depth. (Muldoon's mirror exercise is a really excellent preliminary to this technique since it familiarizes you with your own appearance.)

It is perfectly acceptable to visualize yourself as you are in reality – i.e. dressed in sweater and jeans, or whatever – but some romantic souls find it easier, or possibly just more fun, to see themselves as a mysteriously robed and hooded figure. That is okay too, but pay attention to detail – mysteriously robed and hooded figures do *not* all look the same.

Spend as much time as you need to build up this imaginary figure fully. A good idea is to set aside a particular time each day for the exercise and devote 10 to 15 minutes daily to it for a week or more. Avoid rushing this preliminary stage: it is actually the most important part of the whole exercise, the creation of the 'Body of Light' after which it is named. As you practise, you will find the visualization becomes progressively easier until a simple effort of will is enough to call it up in its entirety. Once you have reached this stage, proceed to phase two of the exercise.

Phase two involves you imagining that you are rising from your chair and walking around the room. Close your eyes and try it out. Remember how the room appears from the viewpoint of your chair, close your eyes and try to visualize that same scene. If you find the details difficult, open your eyes again for a refresher. Keep working at it until you are perfectly capable of describing the room in detail with your eyes closed.

With this achieved, imagine yourself rising from your chair and walking slowly round the edges of the room in a clockwise direction. Try to see in your mind's eye how the perspective of the room changes as you move. Try to remember those small objects and ornaments which were not necessarily visible from your chair, but which you know to be in the room nonetheless.

If you have difficulty with this part of the exercise, open your eyes, stand up *physically* and walk clockwise around the room. Then sit down, close your eyes again, and try to duplicate the journey in your imagination. Keep working on it until your visualization becomes easy and vivid. Now try the same walk anti-clockwise.

After a time – and how much time varies with the individual – you will discover the visualization no longer requires much effort. When this happens, try visualizing yourself in *another* room, again walking around it first clockwise, then anti-clockwise. Select a room you know well, but try visualizing without first visiting it if at all possible.

You should find your mental pictures of the second room come faster and easier than the first since you are, of course, exercising your visualization ability. When you have thoroughly explored the second room, mentally extend your range and visualize yourself wandering throughout your entire house.

Many people visualize extremely well and have little difficulty with any of this. If you are not so fortunate, keep trying: there is no time limit on the exercise and practice will eventually bring it right. Just don't devote more than, say, 20 minutes each day to the practice: this is more than enough, so long as you practise regularly.

The final step in this stage is to imagine yourself exploring some more distant and less familiar scene. Indoors is easier to most people, but if you are feeling really confident, you might try imagining yourself in an outdoor location. Once again, you should explore *methodically*. Avoid visualizing *people* during *any* part of this exercise since this will introduce complications which will slow your progress.

When you are totally happy that you can quickly and easily visualize any area you set your mind to – and visualize it in detail – you are ripe to move on to the final stage of the exercise. This is the crunch. You have now trained yourself to do two things. One is to visualize a sort of mirror image of yourself standing some distance from where you are seated in your chair. The other is to imagine yourself walking around various locations and examining them in detail. For your great leap forward, you are now going to combine the two previous aspects of the exercise.

First, visualize the mirror image of yourself exactly as before. Do this with your eyes open if at all possible. When the figure is definitely there and stable, imagine yourself looking out from its eyes. There is a knack to this, rather like learning to balance on a bicycle. The first few times you try, you will probably fail. But then, for no apparent reason, you will suddenly find you can do it.

Imagine the room from the viewpoint of the figure you have created. Look around and note the details, including your own (physical) body seated in the chair. Once you feel the focus of your perceptions is firmly seated in this imaginary body, have it walk around the room in a clockwise direction, exactly as you did in your imagination during the second stage of the exercise.

Since you have already practised this again and again, you should find it relatively easy to maintain the new perspective. But if you find your consciousness flickering back to where you are sitting in the chair, don't let that worry you. Simply start up again from the beginning.

As you continue with this exercise over a period of time, projecting your focus of consciousness into the imaginary body and having it carry you from room to room, one of two things will happen. Either you will gradually find the reality tone of the experience increases until you can 'see' vividly from the new body, or you will reach a stage where there is a sudden 'jump' after which the experience of the new body seems far more real to you.

At this point, try exploring a totally unfamiliar area while in this imaginary body, then visit the same area when you get back into your physical body. (Which, incidentally, you do by *reversing* the initial process: from the viewpoint of your new body, simply visualize how the room looks from the physical body sitting on the chair.) Do not be *too* shocked if you discover that the scene you saw while in your imaginary body is confirmed in every detail when you visit the spot in reality.

What, you might reasonably wonder, is going on here? If you have successfully followed the technique all the way through, it seems fairly obvious that you have managed to project your consciousness into a second body, that you have, in essence, created a phantom. But while this body can take you anywhere you want to go – and pass through solid walls in the process – it is equally evident that there are substantial differences between the experience and the sort of projections described by people like Monroe and Muldoon.

Where, for example, is the *separation* of one body from the other? In this exercise, you did not actually separate anything from anything – you simply *imagined* a second body standing in the corner. And where was the peculiar state of consciousness apparently so necessary for etheric projection, the hypnogogic boderline between sleep and waking? Where was the physical

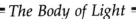

incapacity? You were in a perfectly normal state throughout and if you want to move your physical body you could do so with no trouble whatsoever.

Whatever the similarities, you might be tempted to conclude you were not projecting your etheric body at all. And you would be right. The Body of Light technique brings you closer to something even more exciting than stepping out in your etheric body. It introduces you to astral plane projection.

Part Two
ASTRAL PLANE PROJECTION

1.

Descriptions of an Otherworld

'It seemed to her that she travelled to the steps of a white stone temple. A colonnade of pillars stretched out on either side of her, giving the building a classical appearance, although there were differences from both Greek and Roman architecture.

'She climbed the steps – seven in all – and stood upon a terrace. I suggested to her that she went directly to the library . . . This she did, finding it housed in a room on the left. To my surprise . . . three people were waiting for her there: two men and a woman. The woman appeared in her mid-forties, with calm features and lightly coloured hair – the type that could be blonde or silver. It was the woman to whom Josephine paid most attention, but she noticed all three wore plain, white tunics.

'They were standing at a table and registered Josephine's appearance almost immediately. Although there was no communication, she felt welcome. When Josephine told me of these presences, I assumed . . . that they were librarians – or at least might help her use the store of information in the library. I suggested that . . . she could have the choice of reading from books or viewing their contents on a screen. She opted for the latter, and the location of the screen, high up on one wall, was pointed out by the figures. Somehow it occurred to Josephine that she could 'think' the contents of any book onto the screen . . . '

The quote is from one of my unpublished files. The question is: where was Josephine? Certainly not in this world. A little earlier, while walking along a desert path, she had decided to create a rose; and thought it into existence, complete with thorns and dew. The plant was still growing in the sand next time she passed that way.

Josephine was not, of course, the only person to find herself . . . elsewhere. Emmanuel Swedenborg, the eighteenth century mystic, recorded this account of what he believed to be a descent into hell:

'I once heard loud shouts which sounded as if they were bubbling up through water from lower regions; and from the left came the shout, 'Oh, how just!', from the right, 'Oh, how learned!', and from behind, 'Oh, how wise!'

'And as I wondered whether there could be any just, learned or wise persons in hell, I strongly desired to see the truth of the matter. A voice from heaven then said to me, 'You shall see and hear.'

'So I departed in the spirit and saw before me an opening which I approached and examined, and behold!, there was a ladder, and by this I descended.

'When I had got down, I saw a plain covered with shrubs intermixed with thorns and nettles. I inquired whether this was hell, and was told it was the lower earth which is immediately above hell.'

More recently, the controversial anthropologist, Carlos Castaneda, recorded details of an extensive series of trips through what he called 'the crack between the worlds', including this interesting description:

'Suddenly the scene became very clear, it was no longer like a dream. It was like an ordinary scene, but I seemed to be looking at it through window glass. I tried to touch a column but all I sensed was that I couldn't move; yet I knew I could stay as long as I wanted, viewing the scene. I was in it and yet I was not part of it.

'I experienced a barrage of rational thoughts and arguments. I was, so far as I could judge, in an ordinary state of sober consciousness. Every element belonged in the realm of my normal processes. And yet I knew it was not an ordinary state.

'The scene changed abruptly. It was night-time. I was in the hall of a building . . . I saw a young man coming out of a room carying a large knapsack on his shoulders . . . He walked by me and went down the stairs. By then I had forgotten my apprehension, my rational dilemmas. ''Who's that guy?'' I thought. ''Why did I see him?'' '

I could, without too much difficulty, fill the rest of this book – and a good many future volumes – with accounts of this type. William Blake, the poet, visited heavenly spheres. Carl Jung, the psychologist, found himself transported to a phantasmagorical region of outer space. Every competent shaman has travelled to 'spirit worlds' and brought back power. In rural Ireland, it is still possible to collect second (and occasionally first) hand reports of visits to a faery underworld.

But is there any mystery to this sort of thing? The 'Josephine' mentioned in my opening account was in a hypnotic trance when she visited her temple and grew her rose. Castaneda's experience arose after he took peyote, a powerful plant hallucinogenic. Swedenborg was a prey to visions. And mental hospitals are filled with patients who live in worlds of wonder.

More to the point, there is not one of us who does not visit strange dimensions every night, remembered fleetingly as dreams. Worse, most people have the ability to create pictures *inside their heads*. In some people – novelists, graphic artists, inventors – such pictures can be very vivid and detailed.

Against this background, it seems clear that accounts of visits to strange and alien dimensions are actually *subjective visions*. They are constructs of the human mind, waking dreams conditioned by the individual's personal concerns and cultural milieu. In this context, it is relevant that Swedenborg, an engineer and geologist, was also the son of a Bishop and underwent an ecstatic religious conversion at the age of 56. Blake claimed his own visions sprang from his imagination. They were, he said tapping his forehead, 'in there.'

And yet . . . anthropologist Michael Harner of the School for Social Research in New York ingested a sacred drink made from the 'soul vine' *ayahuasca* while working with the Peruvian Amazon Conibo people.

'Ayahuasca is well known,' writes Dr Lyall Watson. 'It is a woody vine which contains a number of alkaloids with hallucinogenic properties – one of which has been called 'telepatin' because it seems to turn those around you to glass, so that you can see through their bodies and read their minds. I have tried it in Brazil and can vouch for this effect.'

Harner experienced something rather different. He had visions of soul boats, crocodile demons and bird-headed humans. While the experience was vivid and disturbing, Harner had no doubt it was subjective. He knew where the imagery came from. Even superficial analysis indicated similarities to the *Book of Revelation*. He concluded the action of the drug had unlocked strata of his own unconscious and released a string of associations related to his own background and culture.

It was a reasonable assumption, but it was wrong. For Harner subsequently met an old, blind, Amazonian shaman who was able to tell him exactly what he had seen – from the shaman's own experience. They had both visited the same visionary territory. 'I was stunned,' Harner said.

This is a disturbing case – all the more so because it is only one among many . . . and not all of them involving barefoot shamans. During esoteric experimentation, I have had the curious experience of 'looking into' other people's visions and accurately determining the 'dream' environment in which they were operating and the things they were doing. I have also met individuals who could do the same in reverse – telling me details of what I believed to be a personal, subjective fantasy.

Although it is still a long way from attracting the attention of psychologists, scientists or even occultists, the explosive growth in role-play gaming since the middle 1970s had dramatically increased the incidence of 'shared vision.' Typically, half a dozen or so participants in a role-play game have a particular fantasy environment described to them by a game master. They imagine themselves entering this environment as a group and engaging in various adventures together.

Much of the appeal of role-play lies in the freedon it offers to individual players. Within the rules of the game (which are actually the 'Laws' of the imaginary world) you are free to do anything you like. You can stay with your colleagues or wander off on your own, fight an enemy or run away, develop skills or lazily stagnate. The process of the game is highly interactive. Players state what they have decided to do and the game master tells them the immediate results of their actions. As a result, a very vivid mental picture of the imaginary world is built up. And here, so often it is almost commonplace, a strange phenomenon occurs. A player decides to take a certain course of action and imagines himself beginning to do so. And at that point, *before* he explains his intent to the game master, one or more of his fellow players, locked into the same subjective vision, will 'see' what he is up to.

In my earlier book, *Astral Doorways*, I described how a friend and colleague, the artist Nick Van Vliet, triggered a visionary experience by pressing his forehead against an Irish megalith. As he described what he was seeing, his then wife, Bea, stood beside me several yards away, eyes closed, whispering an accurate description of his inner environment moments in advance of his own words. Once again, we are forced to stop and ask ourselves: what it going on here?

One answer has already been given by Carl Jung, who discovered that psychoanalysis often triggered the emergence of identical dream or visionary symbols in different patients. In a technique called 'active imagination' he invited patients to explore their own unconscious by means of imaginary journeys and found that inner landscapes created by them often had a striking similarity. Broader investigations soon determined that characters and scenes from mythology were still very much alive in human imagination, even among patients who had never been exposed to the myths.

Jung found an explanation for all this strangeness in his theory of the *collective unconscious*. He decided that just as humanity shares a single broad body pattern – head, torso, two arms, two legs etc – so it also shares a single broad mind pattern, possibly based on the overall structure of the physical brain. This pattern manifests subjectively as an experience of *archetypes* – tendencies to form similar pictures, linked with similar emotions at a bedrock level of the psyche.

Jung's theory has been frequently misunderstood. It is all too easy to read it as a sort of pre-existent group mind, perhaps generated by the human race, out of which individual minds emerge like islands from the sea. But Jung's use of the term 'collective' carried no such implication – and therein hung the weakness of his whole idea.

Jung is quite correct in his assertion that all human brains share the same basic structure. They are divided in half and look like a walnut. They are layered in a predictable way and can be divided into similar lobes. But the similarities between any two human brains pale into insignificance when set against their differences. There are physical variations in size and weight, variations in overall shape (determined by the shape of the enclosing skull), variations in development of the various areas. Perhaps more to the point, the active brain is not a lump of meat, but a complex electro-chemical machine, which changes its electro-chemical profile millions of times a minute. From this viewpoint, no two human brains are even remotely similar at any given time.

It seems to me that the physical basis of Jung's collective unconscious must be held suspect. But even if I am wrong, it does not matter. When you compare certain 'visionary' reports, you are not dealing with the sort of parallels that might be based on those broad structural similarities which certainly *do* exist between brains; rather you are dealing with precise, frequent and sometimes ongoing areas of identification between two visions. And you are dealing (if you are prepared to work from the findings of occultism and role play) with *visionary interaction*. This absolutely precludes the sort of collective unconscious Jung postulated – at least as an explanation for the phenomenon.

There is possibly another explanation, if not for every anomaly in visionary experience, at least for some. In the study mentioned earlier, triggered by hypnosis, the subject Josephine was temporarily unable to differentiate between her vision and waking reality. She found herself in an environment that looked solid and felt normal, but refused to obey the rules. She could mould matter just by thinking about it. Gravity was present, but obligingly permitted her to fly. There was no familiar cycle of day and night: some areas were in sunshine, others in moonlight . . .

Occultists reading the full account might spot the tell-tale clues. Elements of Josephine's account suggest that, however she got there, she was visiting the Astral Plane.

2.

A Model of the Astral Plane

In *Astral Doorways*, I tried to explain the Astral Plane using a diagram like this:

mental world   self   physical world

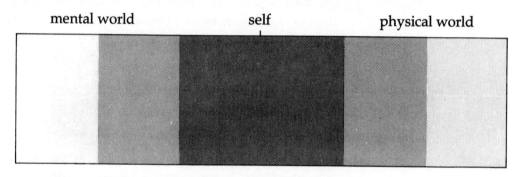

I am not sure I did a particularly good job, but I am certainly willing to give it another try – using the same diagram.

The problem is that the diagram represents an unfamiliar model of the mind. Most of us have become accustomed to thinking of the mind in Freudian terms, with the conscious/unconscious id/ego/superego subdivisions overlaid by an almost instinctive conviction that the mind is somehow not quite *real* – or at least not real in the way the physical world is real.

Scientists are among those who have fallen prey to the conviction. Behaviourism suggests our perception of an inner world is actually an illusion, generated by nothing more than a complex pattern of innate and learned responses to stimuli. Even outside of Behaviourism, there are few scientists prepared to consider the mind distinct from the body. Whatever its structure, most believe it is essentially something created by the electrical impulses of the brain, 'given off', as it were like steam given off by a kettle. I fear you are going to have to forget all that nonsense if you are to understand the Astral Plane.

Look at the diagram and you will notice that it does not show *mind* at all, but rather a *mental world*. This world is not created, caused, or given off by the physical. In fact, the mental world is not even distinct from the physical: the two form an overall *continuum*.

The idea is neither arbitrary nor particularly occult. Those most pragmatic of all scientists, the physicists, have been having a hard time lately coming to terms with what *matter*, the building block of the physical world, might actually be. In the old days it was easy. Matter was something you could drop on your foot. It had mass; it had weight. If you dropped it on your foot, it had momentum. It was capable of *measurement*. Any fool could see it was actually *there*. Most fools could also see it was a very different thing from, for instance energy.

There was a notion about that if you took a lump of matter and cut it into smaller and smaller bits, you would eventually come down to a bit so small you could not cut it any more. The Greeks named this smallest possible lump of matter the *atom*. It was when scientists discovered you could actually crack open an atom that the trouble started. Because what they found in there was no longer matter at all. Worse, it soon turned out to be no longer reasonable.

Sub-atomic physics is an Alice-in-Wonderland world of empty spaces and things called particles which could be thought of as tiny cannon-balls, but could equally accurately be thought of as wave-forms. The trouble is, particles change their behaviour if you look at them, and some of them even go backwards in time. It is a world of weirdnesses like the Uncertainty Principle that says when you get down to individual particles, there is *no way* to predict their behaviour. Thus the entire structure of the physical world is based on nothing more secure than a statistical probability. We do not *think* it will fall apart within the next five seconds . . . but it might.

If you have problems coming to grips with these sort of concepts, imagine how the physicists must have felt. Historically, they had entered a discipline that once promised to weigh and measure the universe. Now it was telling them the universe was hardly there at all. Coming to terms meant the development of new concepts. One prominent scientist suggested the universe was less like a giant machine (the Newtonian model) than a giant thought.

This is something more than analogy. One of the most remarkable collaborations in scientific history was that of Carl Jung, the psychologist, and Wolfgang Pauli, the leading physicist of his day. Specifically, they worked to produce the theory of *synchronicity* which suggests an acausal connecting principle might be abroad in nature. On the way, they came to adopt a viewpoint which holds that mind is the 'reverse side' of matter or, more properly, that mind and matter are the obverse of the same coin – in other words, the universe is a mind/matter continuum.

Standing centred in that continuum is the thing I have labelled **Self** in the diagram. That is you . . . and me as well, of course. According to this model, any one of us is a *focus of consciousness* (and several other things which we will examine in a moment) capable of looking one way into the physical world and looking another way into the mental world.

Generally, while you are awake and active, you are a Janus-headed individual – that is, you continually look both ways at once. You can test the truth of this quite easily with a little self-observation. At this moment you are looking out into a physical world which includes, among other things, your copy of the *Astral Projection Workbook*. But even as you do so, you are watching a reflection of the printed words on an inner screen, part of the mental world. If I start to describe a scene with rivers, lakes and mountains you may even start to see a reflection of that scene in the inner world as well. But the Janus-headed condition is by no means permanent. It is possible for your focus of consciousness to become so intrigued by one world or the other that it *moves into* that world and temporarily loses touch with its counterpart.

A movement of consciousness into the physical world might typically occur at some exciting sporting event, like a soccer match or the Wimbledon tennis championships. As a participant, or observer, your attention is so absorbed by what is going on in the physical world that you lose awareness of the mental world. Obviously you do not cease to think – it would be impossible to play tennis (and probably even soccer) if you did. What is lost is not *mentation*, something often confused with the mental world, but an aspect of your *perception* which would otherwise stare across inner vistas.

This becomes clearer when you recall what happens to you every night. As sleep claims you, your perception of the physical world ceases and you move further into the mental world. Dream landscapes open up, clear-cut perceptions which (at the time you perceive them) are obviously as real as anything you have ever experienced. Orthodox psychology assumes dreamscapes are *processes* rather than places, but even orthodox psychology does not suggest the dreaming process absorbs your whole mental capabilities. Observably, you can still *think* in dreams, albeit perhaps a little less rationally than you do in waking life. A little later you will discover you can actually *wake up* in dreams, think clearly . . . and still continue dreaming.

The notion of a mental world which you can observe and in which you can function is not put forward as an ultimate truth. It is no more than a model – and a pretty simplistic model at that. But as a model it expresses very clearly something I believe to be both factual and important – the objective reality of a dimension other models equate with individual mental processes.

I shall now do a little fancy footwork and extend the model. But first, I need to relabel the diagram. Although the *meaning* and the *explanation* of the diagram have not changed, I think it might be more accurate and certainly would be less confusing if it was labelled like this:

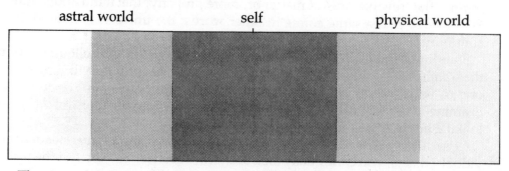

| astral world | self | physical world |

The new label on the left indicates that while there is an inner, finer, intangible aspect of physical reality, a mind-side of matter, which we can (and do) sense by looking inwards, this part of the continuum should never be confused with our own subjective processes.

To call it the 'Mental World' as I did earlier means only that this aspect of reality is analogous with the human mind and can be *sensed* by our mental processes, not that it is those processes themselves. Hopefully, the change of label to 'Astral World', will make sure no confusion arises. Once again, the Astral World is the inner, mind-side of matter, an aspect of an overall continuum. It may be *perceived* by your mind, it may also (as we shall see in a moment) be *influenced* by your mind, but it is certainly not the *same thing* as your mind. So where does your mind actually come in? For that I need a diagram that did not appear in *Astral Doorways*:

self
MIND

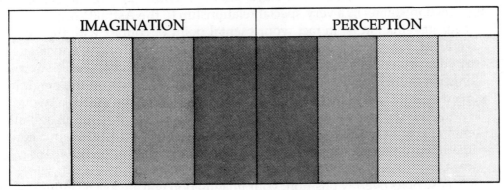

Astral   Physical

The lower portion of the diagram in no way differs from the diagram we have already studied. It shows the continuum from the finer astral world of mindstuff through to the universe of physical matter. But now we have a somewhat different representation of the Self, that focus of consciousness which stands between the two worlds. This may actually be a good time to look more closely at the Self, which has so far been described only as a focus of consciousness, but is, even in our new model, a great deal more. The Self is the totality of what you are. One aspect of it has extension into the physical world – the bit you call your body. One aspect of it processes perceptions of both the outer (physical) and inner (astral) worlds – the bit you call your mind.

Within this model, your mind is seen in fairly orthodox terms. It has conscious and subconscious aspects. It has – or may have, for all I know – those structures like id, ego, libido, superego etc., of which Freud wrote. What it does *not* have is a collective unconscious. Jung's remarkable idea was a mistaken attempt to explain his observations of the Astral World. Much of the inner, Astral World behaves as Jung observed his collective unconscious to behave. And Jung, to his credit, insisted the experience of the collective unconscious was objective, not subjective. But he still believed the collective unconscious was essentially a realm trapped inside your skull, a reflection of the basic pattern of the brain. In fact it was genuinely 'out there', a dimension of the physical universe that all of us experience, consciously or otherwise.

If you examine our latest diagram, you will see that the Mind aspect of the Self has extension in two directions. Over to the right, it extends into the physical world by reason of its *perceptions*. This is just a fancy way of saying the input of your senses allows your mind to examine the physical world and participate in it, by way of your physical body. To the left top of the diagram is the mind's extension inwards, labelled 'imagination'. This is particularly interesting, if only because imagination is a faculty which is almost universally devalued by the various schools of orthodox psychology. Imagination is your ability to make mind pictures, to visualize, to daydream. It can be – and often is – a purely subjective process. But, as I have tried to show in the diagram, your imagination stands in a very special relationship to the Astral World.

Your imagination is, in fact, your mental point of contact with the astral. It 'overlooks' the Astral World in a way similar – but certainly not identical – to the way your perceptions overlook the physical. Your imagination lies, so to speak, alongside the Astral World; or, as I have chosen to show it in the diagram, is spread over it like a blanket. A closer analogy still might be that of a layer of oil floating on the surface of the sea. The layer of oil is your imagination, something quite different from the sea with its own structures, but equally something so profoundly influenced by the sea that it takes on the shape of the waves.

Because of its overlay position, your imagination will always be influenced by events in the Astral World, but for most people the influence is experienced only at an unconscious level. With training, however, your imagination can be turned into a sort of seeing eye, which will allow you to observe astral events quite consciously.

Thus you are born with a mind which is equipped with two distinct data-gathering faculties – your senses and your imagination. Once you leave the womb, your senses are trained and exercised to do their job efficiently, so that throughout your life they continually feed data to your mind for processing. There is an evolutionary urgency about the exercise of your senses, since you would be utterly unable to survive without them.

No such urgency exists in relation to the training of your imagination as a data-gatherer. Most people can – and do – survive perfectly well without exercising their imagination in this way at all. So it is no surprise to discover that the average person has no perception of the Astral World: the inner eye of the imagination has never been trained to see it. Without knowledge of its natural linkage to the Astral World, the imagination itself is devalued. The term 'imaginary' has come to describe that which is essentially unreal and consequently worthless. Fortunately it is never too late to train the inner sense – something you will be doing later in this workbook.

3.

Imagination and its Influence

Unless you are a sub-atomic physicist, your perceptions do not directly influence the outside world. If you want to move mountains, you have to persuade your physical body to co-operate in the job. But just as events in the Astral World impress themselves on your imagination (thus allowing your imagination to be trained for use as an organ of perception) so do the constructs of your imagination impress themselves on the Astral World. This is one of the most important doctrines of traditional occultism – and a concept with far-reaching implications. It is actually the underpinning of almost all magical practice in the Western Esoteric Tradition, and a knowledge of it will save you a great deal of confusion when you undertake astral plane projection.

It seems likely that the reason your imagination can influence the Astral World is that they are actually two of a kind. Some of the very oldest occult schools refer to the astral as the Imagination of the World, or, more accurately, the Imagination of Matter. This is essentially the same idea we have already studied via my little diagrams: the notion that the universe has its mental aspect, which occultists have labelled the Astral Plane. But the idea extends in importance, for we are examining literal, not symbolic, realities.

As part of the physical universe, you too have your own astral aspect, part of which you perceive as your imagination. But your imagination is under the direction of the Self. You can mould it into any shape you wish – and routinely do so every time you day-dream. Since the wider, objective Astral World resonates to your subjective imagination, creations of your imagination will automatically be reflected in the Astral World. Not very clearly, to be sure, and for not very long, at least as far as most people are concerned, but you can train yourself to improve your performance; and there are ways of using the human imagination to influence the Astral World profoundly and permanently.

It may have struck you by this stage that if your personal imagination is simply the subjective experience of your own astral aspect, then an examination of imagination should give you some idea of what the Astral World itself is like. And this is, in fact, the case.

Very many of the older grimoires avoid the terms Astral World or Astral Plane in favour of the term Astral Light. This has followed the experience of mystics, magicians and other astral travellers who have found that beneath the superficial appearance of the Astral World, the ultimate reality was billows of light which had formed themselves into various environments. This does not detract from the reality of the environments any more than the discoveries of sub-atomic physics (which show matter to be largely empty space) detract from the fact that a roof above your head will normally keep out the rain. But a realization that you are essentially dealing with Astral Light certainly prepares you for one of the most peculiar characteristics of the Astral World – its malleable fluidity.

If you want to build a wall around your (physical) back garden, you take on quite a lot of work. You have to buy and stack the necessary bricks. You have to bring in sand, water and cement to mix your mortar. Then you have to lay one brick on top of the other in a special way and stick them together using the mortar you have made. Even then, if you fail to do it just right, there is a good chance your wall will fall down. All this indicates that if you want to make any change in the physical world, you are going to have to invest a lot of energy and effort. We are all so accustomed to the problem that we scarcely stop to think about it, but the physical world is remarkably resistant to change. Look at the heavy machinery we were forced to invent for something as simple as laying a road. The direct opposite is the case in the Astral World. The 'matter' which comprises the astral is so plastic, so fluid, so easily shaped that you can change it with little more effort than a thought.

Think about the way your imagination works. As you sit down to enjoy a good day-dream, you conjure up an imaginary environment. The champagne, cigars and Rolls Royce appear by magic, as does the handsome companion with whom to share them. Almost no effort is involved unless, like an author or painter, you want to increase detail and reality tone, at which point the process becomes hard work – but hard only because all creativity is hard. If you find it difficult to mould a life-like head in clay, the problem is your ability, not the clay.

However clearly the term 'Astral Light' expresses this underlying malleability, I dislike it because it gives the impression that the Astral Plane is a featureless and formless area, like looking into fog or clouds. The reality is very different. Cast your mind back to that earlier abstract from my records of Josephine's astral experiences. There was ground beneath her feet and sky above her head. There were growing plants and desert sands. There was a building. There were people. Nothing at all formless here. Indeed, by carefully selecting the quotes, I might easily have given you the impression she was on holiday in Greece.

How does this tally with the 'astral billows' spoken of by, among others, the French magus Eliphas Levi? The fact is, the astral billows exist only in the way that electrons, neutrons and positrons exist – as part of a background of which very few of us ever become personally aware. You may learn that the Astral Plane is actually the Astral Light, but you will never experience it that way. What you will experience is strange landscapes in which the wall around your back garden is a great deal easier to build. The landscapes and structures of the Astral Plane arise from a multiplicity of causes.

First, there are reflections of the physical world. Physical features seem to impress themselves on corresponding areas of the astral given enough time. The qualifier is important. The fact you knocked up a tool-shed yesterday will not create an instant astral structure. It requires not merely weeks, or even years, but several centuries before a physical feature will automatically begin to impress itself on the astral. Thus you might find a familiar cathedral on the inner level, but few enough redbrick semi-detached bungalows.

Two factors are required for an impression to form: age and permanence. A building, for example, which is of great age but has been continually modified does not impress itself well. Ancient trees, which are continually modifying themselves by growth, scarcely impress at all. Even something as apparently permanent as a landscape is usually subject to erosion, changes in vegetation, movement of water courses and so on to a degree sufficient to halt the formation of an astral counterpart. But some landscapes do impress. Areas of hard rock, mountain fastnesses, ice-fields and the like all have a good chance of developing astral reflections; and in so doing becoming part of the landscape of the Astral Plane.

Thoughts – or, more accurately, mental pictures – impress themselves on the Astral Light far more easily, as we have already noted. But not so easily as all that. That passing fantasy you had last night will leave no trace (you may be quite relieved to hear). What is required for an impression is that a large number of people concentrate on a single image simultaneously; or that a smaller number concentrate *repeatedly* on the same image. That 'smaller number' may actually shrink to one, but if you are going solo, you will need a trained imagination and a lot of perseverance. Another factor which aids the imprinting process is *emotion*. An emotionally-driven image imprints far more effectively on the astral than any other.

Taking these various factors together, it is possible to predict the sort of imprints that might be made on the Astral Light. First, you will have reflections of various physical environments, characterized by the fact that they have remained unchanged, on the physical plane, for a great many centuries. This category would largely comprise geographical features, but will also include certain man-made structures – e.g. the pyramids at Giza. Next, you have the reflected imagery of certain human group concerns. There has been some reference in occult literature to areas of the 'lower astral' which are supposed to reflect the shibboleths of the human subconscious, dark places full of repressed rage, uncontrollable fears and perverted sexuality.

I have yet to meet anyone who has experienced these areas personally and I have considerable difficulty in accepting their reality. The mechanics that supposedly underlie their formation are frankly wrong. What impresses is a long-standing image, not an amorphous mass of emotions. You might, admittedly, pick up a 'feel' or 'atmosphere' generated by mass emotional response to some human disaster – the misery caused by an Ethiopian famine, for example. But human disasters are self-limiting in time (because the people who endure them die) and emotional response is consequently short lived, so that the chances of permanent imprint are small.

Since the human race as a whole shares very few obsessional images, the most likely impressions tend to arise racially and are usually related to religion, as secular images are frequently too short-lived. At any given time, certain fashions in architecture or art might impress, as might a long-standing political concern, but these will all be unstable in the Astral World and will not long outlast their physical world counterparts. The exceptions are, of course, styles generated by the more enduring civilizations – all of them ancient – like Greece, Rome or China. These will typically outlast their physical manifestations, often by a very long time indeed.

An example of astrally-impressed religious imagery might be a culture's perception of the dwelling place of its gods. Thus one might reasonably expect to find a reflection of Olympus, based on the Greek concept and still surviving long after Ancient Greece has passed away. Our own culture, I suspect, is busily engaged on impressing rather silly pictures of Heaven as a city of clouds and harps, and Hell as a cavern of fiery brimstone.

A step down from racial concerns are group concerns, but here again the imprints tend to be religious – nothing else really provides the single-minded imagery and the emotion combined with the sort of ritualistic concentration which can keep throwing up the same imagery day after day for years. Political or commercial groupings, however traditional, will seldom provide sufficient of the necessary factors for a permanent imprint.

At individual level, few of us have any opportunity to imprint permanently on the astral. But there are four exceptions: the creative artist, the magician, the astral traveller and the mentally-ill obsessive.

To take the latter category first, an emotionally-driven obsessive can sometimes raise sufficient energy and perseverence to imprint the object of his obsession on the Astral Light – an unfortunate development since it will then tend to reinforce the obsession. The other categories are a little more fortunate. The magician is, of course, trained to astral operations. The magical mind is skilled in visualization and concentration; and adept in the techniques of drumming up emotions to fuel a successful imprint. It is a sort of controlled hysteria, but it works.

The creative artist brings other factors into play, in relation to his or her particular speciality. An architect brooding on a house design will, given emotional involvement and clear, detailed visualization, create a temporary imprint which will, however, tend to stabilize once the physical house is built. A popular novelist, by contrast, imprints on the astral through reader assistance. The emotional involvement of millions over a time span of more than a century, make it a safe bet that you could, with luck, meet Mr Pickwick and Sam Weller on the Astral Plane. They would be shells, of course, personality constructs a shade more limited than a genuine article, but you would never think it as you shook hands with them.

The category of astral traveller imprints effectively for reasons I do not entirely understand – indeed, to be honest, for reasons I do not understand at all. But on the basis of experiments, I know that if you can project directly into the astral, you will find it far easier to modify the astral environment than you would from the physical plane. Josephine needed no special training to create her rose. And this brings us to an interesting point. We have seen that your imagination can be trained to *look into* the Astral Plane and even *create structures* on the Astral Plane, but neither ability seems to have very much to do with actually *projecting*. In fact, up to this point, there is nothing we have examined which seems to provide any promising *mechanism* for projection. The whole picture has suggested that you can look and you can manipulate, but you cannot enter.

Yet it obviously *is* possible to enter the Astral Plane. Occultists have talked about doing so for centuries and we already have examined reports from Josephine, Swedenborg and other travellers who claim to have been there. To find out how it was done, take a look now at yet another modification of our familiar diagram:

self

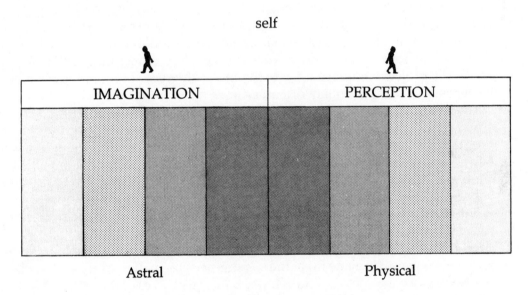

Astral   Physical

Two little figures have been added, one walking towards the right of the picture, the other towards the left. The one on the right symbolizes your physical body, that handsome hunk of muscle, bone and blood which allows you to function in the physical world. The one on the left is a different sort of body altogether – one you never knew you had.

4.

Introducing Your Astral Body

If you read the first part of the workbook before turning to this section, you will already know about your second (etheric) body, an electrical field which provides the pattern for your physical form. You may also recall a passing reference to the fact that you come equipped with several subtle bodies, one inside the other like Russian dolls. And you should remember that final exercise, the Body of Light technique, which enabled something very similar to an etheric projection, but seemed to involve a different sort of 'etheric' vehicle to the one we had previously discussed.

The time has come to admit that the Body of Light technique only *mimics* an etheric projection – it does not actually produce one. What it really does is promote the separation of a different subtle body altogether – the true astral body. This body *can* function on the physical plane; and does so when it simulates an etheric projection. But its real home is the Astral World. It is the vehicle you will use for any full astral plane projection.

The astral body does not appear to be an electrical field – or, indeed, anything easily recognizable to modern science. Occultists say it is made of 'mind stuff', specifically the same 'stuff' you manipulate with every act of visual imagination. This means it is made up of the same superfine 'matter' as the Astral Plane itself. But since we know precious little about the physics of the astral, this does not take us very much further. It is, however, possible to say quite a lot about the astral body on the basis of experience. Certainly it exhibits some very strange characteristics.

During an etheric projection you feel more or less as you do in your physical body, until such time as you decide to wander through a wall. An astral body projection confined to the physical plane can be very similar . . . but equally it can be very different. Cast your mind back to the Body of Light technique. By means of that technique, you created a subtle body for yourself through an act of imagination. We are culturally conditioned to consider anything created by the imagination as essentially unreal, or at very least subjective. There is, however, strong evidence that this is not so.

Madame Alexandra David-Neel, one of the few Westerners to thoroughly explore pre-invasion Tibet and the only woman, so far as I am aware, ever to be made a lama, wrote a fascinating account of something called *tulpa creation*. A tulpa, according to traditional Tibetan doctrines, is an entity created by an act of imagination, rather like the fictional characters of a novelist, except that *tulpas* are not written down. Madame David-Neel became so interested in the concept of the *tulpa* that she decided to try to create one.

The methods involved are not a million miles away from the Body of Light technique in that they are essentially a matter of prolonged, regular concentration and visualization. But whereas with the Body of Light you are merely creating a shell self which you plan to animate at a later stage, the *tulpa* is conceived as a complete personality totally separate and distinct from yourself.

Madame David-Neel's *tulpa* began its existence as a plump, benign little monk, somewhat similar to the popular picture of Friar Tuck. The vision was at first entirely subjective, a visualization that existed purely within her mind. But gradually, with practice, Madame David-Neel was able to visualize the *tulpa* out there, like an imaginary ghost flitting about the real world. In time the vision grew in clarity and substance until she came to see the *tulpa* as solid and objectively real – what Western psychology would call a self-induced hallucination. Whenever she wished to switch it on, there it would be.

However, the day came when the hallucination declined to remain under conscious control. She discovered that the monk would appear from time to time when she had *not* willed it. This was disturbing in itself. Even more so was the fact that her friendly little figure was slimming down and taking on a distinctly sinister aspect. Eventually her companions, who were unaware of the mental disciplines she was practising, began to ask about the 'stranger' who had turned up in their camp – a clear indication that a creature which was no more than solidified imagination had definite objective reality.

But the only difference between the *tulpa* seen by others and the creature first formed in Madame David-Neel's head, was the length and intensity of her concentration. Rationally we have to admit that if the *tulpa* was visible and objective in the latter stages of the exercises, it must have been equally objective – if invisible – at the beginning. This means that the Body of Light you created was objectively real as well. But if this body had substance, it was the substance of imagination – astral substance in other words. Consequently it is reasonable to refer to this body as an astral body. (You may feel inclined to take issue with this reasoning since the Body of Light is entirely artificial, something you literally 'dreamed up' in the course of the exercise. And I have already said that your astral body is one of a series of subtle bodies which form a natural part of your esoteric anatomy. But I have reason to believe the distinction between a home-grown 'natural' astral body and a home-made 'artificial' one is a lot less clear cut than you might think: I did warn you the astral body was weird. In the circumstances, you might perhaps humour me enough to suspend judgement for a while.)

When you created that body and imagined yourself looking at the world through its eyes, there is an excellent chance that the experience was at first little different from the earlier part of the exercise in which you simply imagined yourself walking around the room without reference to any particular astral body. That is to say, you felt as if you were day-dreaming. And at first you may actually have *been* day-dreaming – i.e. engaged in a purely subjective exercise – since it is extremely difficult to differentiate between subjective vision and actual projection in these early stages.

What you were attempting to do in this part of the Body of Light technique was not to project a subtle body at all, but rather to project your *focus of consciousness.* You were, if I may put it this way, trying to float your mind out of your physical body in order that it might *animate* the astral shell you created. With a lot of experience, it is possible to sense the precise point at which you succeed in doing this, but the sensation is extremely subtle. For most people, the only sure way to tell if you are successfully animating an astral shell (as distinct from day-dreaming) is if you can use the shell to bring back information you did not previously know – to walk into a strange room, for example, and accurately determine its contents.

Although an animated astral shell is a valid projection, the subjective experience of this artificial astral body varies very little from an act of imagination. Your body and environment lack reality tone. There is a tendency for the experience to shift, dim and break up altogether, leaving your consciousness firmly back in your physical body.

If you have already managed an etheric projection, you will see the difference at once. Etheric projections are characterized by their sensation of absolute normality. Most inexperienced projectors assume they are still in the physical body until something (like my experience of the unco-operative doorknob) forces them to accept they are not. But if you continue to practise projecting your consciousness into this astral shell, the time comes when something very exciting happens. The experience takes on the same reality tone as an etheric projection. There is no longer any question about whether or not you may be day-dreaming – you know perfectly well you are not.

At that point, so long as you remain alone in a familiar, physical environment, there is not much to distinguish between this experience and a true etheric projection. What has happened is that as well as projecting your focus of consciousness, you managed to project your natural astral body as well. It coincided with the created astral shell and merged with it. But note that word 'alone' in the sentence about distinguishing between the two types of projection. When you project your astral body to mimic etheric projection, your *range of perception* is greater than when you are locked into your etheric body. Specifically, you are able to see entities at your own level of being – i.e. astral entities. As a result, astral body projections of this sort sometimes end up in confusion as the projector discovers he can see people – and sometimes creatures – who he knows are not there.

I had an example of this phenomenon with the same Arthur Gibson I mentioned in the first section of this workbook. On what was obviously an astral body projection mimicking an etheric projection, he successfully described portion of the interior of a strange house but met (and talked to!) an individual he assumed to be the owner. Subsequent investigation soon indicated the individual did not exist . . . at least on the physical plane.

Less often, your extended perception will create a sort of overlay effect in which your potential awareness of the Astral Plane is, so to speak, *superimposed* on the physical. The result can be very confusing as familiar surroundings take on an unfamiliar aspect. Several of Robert Monroe's projection descriptions read suspiciously as if he was experiencing this effect. It is incidentally, quite possible to obtain a very similar experience within the context of an astral plane projection. The plane, as we have already noted, is extremely malleable – so much so that some people actually seem able to mould its shapes *unconsciously*. If you are one of them, and particularly if you are unfamiliar with astral plane projection, you may find yourself creating a familiar physical scene in such detail that you mistake it for the real thing. But it is not the real thing, so that astral entities may enter or leave your construct at will.

The merging of your true astral body with the shell you created is a painless experience with one interesting aspect: you will normally take on the shape of the artificial body. Obviously, if you created this body to look like your own, the merging produces nothing of note. But if you created a distinctly different shape – the sinister hooded figure, for example – then that, for the duration of the projection, will be the form of your astral body. From this, you will readily deduce that your astral body shares the peculiar fluidity common to the plane itself. If you have ever wondered what it was like to be a werewolf, then an astral body projection is an excellent time to find out, for once you recognize the possibility, you can shape-shift at will.

In one of his occult romances, Dennis Wheatley described how the villain chased the hero (each in his respective astral body) through the billows of the Astral Light. Both shape-shifted shamelessly as the chase proceeded: the hero became a fly to escape a net . . . the villain became a bird to eat the fly . . . the hero became a snake to kill the bird . . . and so on. All sterling stuff for a thriller and if the description was a little bit over the top, the basic principle was sound – on the Astral Plane or, more accurately, within your astral body, you can take on any shape you wish. This might lead you to believe your astral body has no essential shape of its own – and indeed there are reports from some projectors of trips through the Astral Plane in bodies so bereft of distinguishing features that they appeared as balls of light. Yet my own experience clearly suggests your astral body *does* have a specific shape to which it will naturally revert if you leave it alone.

While the astral remains coincident with the physical, etheric and other subtle vehicles, there is no problem at all. Each one is – more or less – the mirror image of the other. The qualification in parentheses arises out of a long-standing suspicion that body image may be more closely associated with the astral body than the physical. It is by no means unusual for individuals to retain a subjective picture of their own bodies which differs – and sometimes differs susbtantially – from the reality. This body image has actually been measured. Volunteers in a series of ingenious experiments were invited to study themselves in a variety of *distorting* mirrors and indicate which image looked most life-like.

The investigators discovered that with some subjects, there was a marked difference between the selected image and the reality of their physical bodies. It is a finding my own experience as one-time director of a weight-loss clinic bears out. At that time, I was well accustomed to clients whose perception of their physical weight, shape and bulk was often grossly inaccurate. On one occasion, a young professional woman so thin she might have been a famine victim told me seriously she was 'like an elephant.' It may be that some distortion of the astral body produces imagery like this. Alternatively, imagery like this is almost certain to produce some distortion of the astral body. Either way, it leaves a subtle vehicle which is *not* a double of the physical.

Once you succeed in projecting into the Astral Plane, my experience has been that your astral body *never* mirrors the physical. Why this should be I have no idea, but it is borne out by direct observation.

The variation is extreme and could not be described as any sort of body-image distortion. In one case that comes to mind, the projector was a small, blonde-haired, blue-eyed woman with a squarish build and clearly-defined features. Her astral body was black-haired, brown-eyed, of average height and slightly plumpish build. It also gave the appearance of a younger woman by perhaps as much as 20 years.

My own astral body differs just as substantially from the physical in that it too gives a younger appearance, is clean-shaven (where I have been bearded since the age of 17) marginally taller and definitely plumper than I am, with softer features. Nor does it wear glasses, as I have been forced to do since the age of 12, although I cannot, I suppose, rule out the possibility of astral contact lenses.

How or why the differences arise I have no idea, but the position is further confused by the surprising factor of instant recognizability. During an astral plane projection any friends you meet may look very different to the way they do in their physical bodies, but you will recognize them instantly. Once again, I do not know how or why, although the phenomenon obviously raises the suspicion that we may all be far more familiar with this sort of experience than we think. This is by no means an outlandish suggestion. There is at least some evidence to suggest we may be capable of simultaneous function on astral and physical planes with each of the two bodies giving every indication of conscious mentation and neither, apparently, aware of the activities of the other. This sort of unconscious inter-dimensional bi-location strikes me as a promising field for investigation, but you will be relieved to hear I do not propose to investigate it here.

Another school of thought suggests that dreaming is astral plane projection while unconscious; a theory difficult either to disprove or prove. As we have seen in Section One, some projectors, like Sylvan Muldoon, consider certain dreams to be muddled recollections of *etheric* projections. The two ideas are not, of course, mutually exclusive; and if dreams really *are* examples of regular astral plane projections, it would certainly explain why we recognize friends so easily on the astral levels, even though their appearance can differ substantially from what we are used to on the physical.

Curiously, since the literature of occultism is vast and the concept of the astral body ancient, there are remarkably few really detailed accounts either of this subtle body or of the physics of the Astral Plane. But perhaps you will not need them, since there is a wealth of available information on the mechanics of astral plane projection – something which, hopefully, you will soon be trying for yourself.

5.

Lucid Dreams

In the introduction to a short, useful book entitled *Lucid Dreaming*, Gregory Scott Sparrow has this to say:

'For decades . . . Western metaphysical and occult literature has been discussing astral projection and out-of-body experience. However, the one-sided approach which characterized these early writings was one of trying to determine *where* the soul or entity was going. Underlying this approach was an emphasis on *physically* leaving one's present circumstances in the body and the world. In these writings there was a tendency to regard the environment of the out-of-body experience as actually existing somewhere in time and space.

'The term 'lucid dreaming' represents an entirely different orientation to the same experience. Instead of implying that a person is physically escaping the confines of the body, this orientation focuses upon the fact that self-reflecting consciousness is functioning without the apparent mediation of the body; thus it leaves open the possibility that the dreamer has transcended time and space. Consequently, all that is left to really talk about is the dreamer's own state of self-conscious awareness during the experience, which has been termed ''lucidity.''

'Of course, the lucid dreamer then tends to make conclusions about *where* he may be (e.g. out of the body, on the astral plane). But these conclusions are mere speculations and can lead to all kinds of intricate systems describing the *physical* process of the soul's leaving and re-entering the body. This avoids the possibility that the 'projector' is within *himself* and that this other world which he sees is an outgrowth of his own past attitudes and experiences.'

I hardly need tell you I disagree with most of this. Since etheric and astral phantoms have been seen by others and the same astral plane environments visited by different voyagers, it seems quite clear that 'physically leaving one's present circumstances in the body and the world' is exactly what is happening.

Nor would I agree this avoids the possibility that the world a projector sees is an outgrowth of his own past attitudes and experiences. The structure of the

Astral Plane is such that it might very well be. The Astral Light is sufficiently malleable to take on any shape unconsciously imposed on it by creative projectors and in that sense is certainly an outgrowth of the projector's past attitudes and experiences. This does not make it a subjective world, merely an objective world oddly reflective of subjective states. But for all this, lucid dreaming is a good place to start experimenting with the Astral Plane. If the pundits are right – and I have every reason to believe they might be – then you are *already* an astral plane projector who travels unconsciously to the strange Otherworld at night.

The catch-22 keyword is, of course, the term *unconsciously*. Dreams can be great fun while they are going on, but they are things that *happen to you*. You have no (conscious) control of your (astral) environment in a dream. It shifts and changes fitfully, creating that fluidity so characteristic of dreams. And the experience is one of deception. During a dream, you are not typically aware of the fact that you are dreaming, not typically aware of the fact that you have projected into a new world. Instead, you thoughtlessly presume the action is taking place somewhere in the physical world you lived in during daylight hours – however unlikely this might be. After the event, on waking, the dream is, of course, recognized for what it was. But the memory of its detail quickly fades. Most dreams are lost within minutes of waking. In many cases, post-waking amnesia is so profound that the individual is convinced she never dreams at all.

If dreams of this sort do represent astral plane projection, then they are projections which differ only technically from subjective visions. In them, the astral environment is shaped entirely by your unconscious mind, the events which occur are dramatizations of your unconscious concerns, the people you meet are personifications of your own psychic processes. The fact that you are manipulating an astral environment is irrelevant. In practical terms, the dreamscape might have been created by the firing of electrical impulses within your brain. *Lucid* dreaming is something else.

Scott Sparrow defines lucid dreaming quite simply as a dream in which the dreamer becomes conscious. This sounds a little like Sylvan Muldoon's etheric projection technique in which self-suggestion triggers a wake-up process at a predetermined point in a projection dream. But the two things are, in fact, entirely different. Muldoon's technique was aimed at breaking the dream and making you conscious of your projection in the physical world. Sparrow's definition means only that you become *conscious* you are dreaming. The dream itself remains intact and you *do not* wake up.

Because of your general familiarity with the dream state, becoming conscious within a dream is an excellent introduction to the Astral Plane. Almost your first thought is likely to be the recognition that you are now in total control of your environment and can go anywhere, do anything you wish. The sense of freedom is dramatic.

Since the Astral Plane is both extensive and objective, the sensation of omnipotence which usually follows is ultimately an illusion, but it does at least allow you to start out learning about the plane without panic. Panic on the

Astral Plane is a greater problem than it is on the physical plane – and it can cause quite enough trouble even there! Because of its reflective nature, the plane will all too easily allow you to confront your fears *objectively* – something which can be extremely unpleasant at the best of times; and absolutely terrifying if you are unprepared or, worse, do not realize what is happening.

In *Astral Doorways* I remarked that if you meet anything nasty on the astral, it is because there is something nasty inside you. This was a slight overstatement, since there *are* objective nasties on the plane which exist in their own right or are generated by others. But as a general rule of thumb, anything you meet is either self-*created* or self-*attracted*. That latter point is important. A self-created environment will not only reflect your unconscious needs, fear and desires directly, but will also *attract* objective entities of a like nature. To function really effectively on the Astral Plane, you will need to take responsibility not only for your actions, but for your character and emotions as well.

Edgar Cayce, America's famous sleeping prophet, was once asked 'What governs the experiences of the astral body while in the fourth dimensional plane during sleep?' His reply, although confusing in its phraseology, under-lines the point I have been making:

'This is, as has been given, that upon which it has fed. That which it has builded; that which it seeks; that which the mental mind, the subconscious mind, the subliminal mind, *seeks!* That governs . . . '

In other words, on the astral, you will find everything you are unconsciously seeking, good or bad. Perhaps fortunately, *total* control of your astral environment is unusual (indeed, may not actually be possible) and environmental reflection of your unconscious state does not always happen, except in a very general way. But before any of these things become a real concern to you, there is the obvious problem of becoming conscious within a dream. Most people, sooner or later, will experience a dream in which the possibility that they are dreaming occurs to them by accident. Unfortunately such a realization almost invariably breaks the dream and causes them to awaken. The trick is to trigger such a realization without breaking the dream. There are quite a number of techniques available for doing so.

Your first major step is to pay more *attention* to your dreams. Our culture has convinced most of us that dreaming is a waste activity of no importance whatsoever, a sort of side-show put on by the brain as it seeks to clear itself of toxins accumulated during the day. Older, perhaps wiser, cultures paid far more attention to dreams, believing that they might be vehicles of prophecy or messages from divinities. Whatever about these beliefs, dreams have a definite importance to anyone with ambitions to become an astral plane projector and are consequently well worth the effort of study.

One way of studying your dreams is to keep a notebook or cassette recorder next to your bed and record their content immediately on waking. It is not easy to do. For most people, the last thing they need is mental effort first thing in the morning. But if you are strong-willed and if you persevere, it eventually gets to be a habit, hence easier. Failing the notebook approach, it is still useful to set aside a few minutes each morning – as early as possible – to make a conscious effort at recalling your dreams of the night before. What you are looking for, in the early stages, is any indication of *pre-lucid* dreaming.

A pre-lucid dream is one in which you dream that you are waking up, without, however, actually doing so. I want to be clear about this: in a pre-lucid dream, you dream that you wake up out of a dream, but do not awaken in actuality, nor do you become conscious that you are dreaming. Most people have such dreams from time to time, but having one in the present circumstances is not entirely a matter of luck. As you begin to actively study your dreams with the intention of experiencing lucid dreaming, you automatically increase the chances of such an experience. (The psychological mechanics are clear enough: by brooding about lucid dreams, you give your unconscious mind an automatic suggestion that it should produce a few.)

Pre-lucid dreams are a move along the road towards lucid dreaming and often have a remarkable clarity and reality tone in their own right. But they are still not lucid dreams: they do not permit you to realize you are dreaming. Nonetheless, their appearance is a clear indication that you are beginning to get results. You can speed the process in a couple of ways. Sparrow discovered there was a relationship between lucid dreaming and meditation:

'When lucidity began to arise with increasing regularity in the following months, I soon noticed that it emerged predictably after a deep and fulfilling meditation. It became clear that when my devotional life was intense, lucid dreams would arise as a concomitant. This relationship became more pronounced when I began meditating for 15 or 20 minutes during the early morning hours (from 2:00 to 5:00 a.m.)'

He concluded that diligent meditation in the early morning hours for the purpose of *attunement* would result in lucid dreaming, but warns that meditating for the purpose of *obtaining* a lucid dream is unlikely to succeed. His own attempts to do so consistently ended in failure and he frequently had dreams which told him not to do it. The point is subtle enough to warrant repeating. Early morning meditation for the purpose of, say, spiritual advancement, tends to be followed by lucid dreaming as a sort of side-effect. Early morning meditation for the purpose of triggering a lucid dream does not work.

I should, I suppose, make the point that, to judge from his written work, Scott Sparrow is an individual deeply concerned with spirituality and Christian ideals. He clearly believed initially – and possibly still believes – that lucid dreams were in the nature of a 'gift'. 'I remember lying in my bed bewildered, wondering why the experience had been given to me and what I had done to deserve it,' he wrote in *Lucid Dreaming*. He concluded on this occasion that it had followed on an unselfish act towards his brother and that 'unselfish acts had been a rarity in my life.' Following on his early experience, he noted that lucidity often arose after an experience of love or deep rapport with another person.

Since I am not a particularly spiritual individual, I find it personally difficult to judge the validity of this relationship, but mention it in the hope that it may be of use to some readers. The effect of meditation is, however, extremely interesting and has a far more universal application since almost any form of meditation, properly performed, tends to put you in close touch with your essential self – which I suspect is the trigger factor in producing the lucid dreams.

Meditation for the *purpose* of lucid dreaming would automatically set up barriers since it is, in itself, a superficial goal. The result is a little like *trying* to relax. Relaxation is a question of *letting go*. So long as you keep *trying* you will never let go completely. Only when you learn how to stop trying does total relaxation follow. Another trigger is the one put forward in a different context by Sylvan Muldoon – self suggestion. You can apply this immediately before sleep when you are pleasantly relaxed and your unconscious is amenable to doing what it is told. Simply repeat to yourself, over and over, that next time you dream, you will become aware of the fact you are dreaming.

You might try to link this suggestion with a typical dream scenario. This is where your study of your dreams comes into its own, for by this stage you should be well able to isolate recurring – or at least typical – themes. You might, for example, find a great number of your dreams involve walking down a city street. If so, then you should suggest that the next time you dream of walking down a city street, you will become aware that you are dreaming. Since you have a visual image (the street) to work on, it could be useful to make the suggestion in visual form, *imagining* yourself dreaming, then becoming aware that you are dreaming. Keep using the suggestion night after night and sooner or later your typical city street pattern will recur, triggering the suggestion. A somewhat different technique waits until you are in the dream itself before trying to trigger awareness. This is done by the oddly simple expedient of examining your hands or some other part of your (dream) body.

Sleep research has indicated that the most predictable element of any dream is the presence your own body. Any examination of it tends to reinforce your sense of personal identity, since it forces your attention away from the swiftly changing astral elements which make up most of the remainder of the dream. Another useful point of focus is the ground beneath your feet, another unchanging element in an otherwise fluid environment.

The problem with both these techniques is quite obvious – the difficulty in remembering to examine your hands or the ground when the dream starts. Here again, a clear, conscious determination prior to falling asleep will help, as will the specific self-suggestion that in any dream from now on you will examine your hands, or the ground beneath your feet. Once more, you have a visual reference, so the self-suggestion can be made visually.

I would strongly suggest you try these approaches for several weeks before giving up on any of them, but if you *do* find yourself getting nowhere with them, you might be prepared to attempt some rather more complex and difficult approaches developed many centuries ago in Tibet. As a result of these methods, says Dr W. Y. Evans-Wentz in his *Tibetan Yoga and Secret Doctrines*, the *yogin* enjoys as vivid a consciousness in the dream state as in the waking state – precisely the condition you are trying to bring about.

The first – and probably least useful – of these methods involves your development of a determination to recognize the ultimate unreality of all things. 'In other words,' quotes Evans-Wentz, 'under all conditions during the day [or waking state] hold to the concept that all things are of the substance of dreams and that thou must realize their true nature.' At night, when on the point of sleep, pray that you will be able to understand the dream state and resolve that you will be able to do so.

The initial concept (that everything is a dream) is heavier going for the products of a Western culture than it is for Tibetans with a centuries-long Buddhist tradition – which teaches as a central article of faith that all is *maya* or illusion. But it may have intellectual or emotional appeal to you, in which case both the nightly prayer (to your *guru,* according to the Tibetan text, but any divinity tends to be just as effective) and the determination to succeed will act as a powerful self-suggestion.

The second practice is rather more mechanical. The text insist it relies on the 'power of breath' although no breath control is actually involved. The translation may be in error to the extent that the 'breath' referred to may be the 'universal breath', or what the Chinese call *ch'i. Ch'i* is a subtle energy found, among other places, in the human body and capable of regulation by the techniques of acupuncture, acupressure, and various yogas and physical fitness systems like *Tai Ch'i.*

The instructions given to stimulate dream understanding by regulation of this energy are fairly straightforward:

1. Sleep lying on your right side.
2. Use the thumb and ring-finger of your right hand to press on the arteries of your throat. (You can tell these by the fact that they have a pulse.)
3. Stop the nostrils with the fingers of the left hand, thus forcing yourself to breathe through your mouth.
4. Allow saliva to collect in the throat.

The last Tibetan practice I plan to discuss here is the most complex of them all, and in some ways the most interesting. You will have to bear with me for a moment as I quote directly from Evans-Wentz translation of the texts:

'Thinking that thou art thyself the deity Vajra-Yogini, visualize in the throat psychic centre the syllable *AH,* red of colour and vividly radiant, as being the real embodiment of Divine Speech.

'By mentally concentrating upon the radiance of the *AH,* and recognizing every phenomenal thing to be in essence like forms reflected in a mirror, which, though apparent, have no real existence of themselves, one comprehendeth the dream.

'At nightfall, strive to comprehend the nature of the dream-state by means of the visualization just described above. At dawn, practise 'pot-shaped' breathing seven times. Resolve 11 times to comprehend the nature of the dream-state. Then concentrate the mind upon a dot, like unto a bony substance, white of colour, situated between the eyebrows.

'If one be of plethoric temperament, the dot is to be visualized as being red of colour; if one be of nervous temperament, the dot is to be visualized as being green of colour.

'If by this means the dream-state be not comprehended, then proceed as followeth:

'At nightfall meditate upon the dot. In the morning, practise 21 'pot-shaped' breathings. Make 21 resolves to comprehend the nature of the dream-state. Then, by concentrating the mind on a black dot the size of an ordinary pill, situated at the base of the generative organ, one will be enabled to comprehend the nature of the dream-state.'

Unless you have had the benefit of esoteric training, parts of that are likely to make very little sense to you. But between us we might manage to extract a useful technique.

The first problem is that phase 'throat psychic centre,' which refers to something usually called a *chakra* or *chakram*. *Chakra* is usually translated as 'lotus' and *chakras* are believed to be subtle centres within every human body which act as transformer stations for the universal power of *prana* or *ch'i*. There is no need to go into any depth examination of the chakras, but take a look at the diagram below:

Five of the major chakras are shown as glowing spheres. The second from the top is the 'throat psychic centre' mentioned in the Tibetan yoga text. My own experience suggests that if it is strongly stimulated, a combined etheric/astral projection results. Milder stimulation, as you may have gathered from the text, is useful in dream control.

One of the simplest, safest, and in many ways most effective ways of stimulating any chakra is visualization. The text requires practitioners to imagine themselves to be the deity Vajra-Yogini, an identification which would certainly boost a Tibetan's confidence in success, but is meaningless for most Westerners. It is an instruction you may safely ignore, as is the bit about the syllable *AH* and the 'real embodiment of Divine Speech' – more religious associations which are generally meaningless to Westerners.

The use of the colour red and visualization concentrated on the throat centre is something else again. Before retiring to bed, take 10 minutes to visualize a glowing blood-red sphere within your throat, its mellow light illuminating that whole area of your body. Do not spend more than 10 minutes since any concentration on a single chakra (in isolation) leads to an unbalanced energy flow and health problems if continued too long. As you visualize, determine that you are going to become aware of dreaming as you dream; and think of the reflective structure of the Astral Plane as outlined earlier in this workbook.

Red is an energizing colour and there is an excellent chance the above exercise is all you will need to get results. But if you carry it out diligently for a week to 10 days without achieving your goal, move on to the second stage.

At night, before falling asleep, proceed exactly as before. But next morning, immediately after you awaken (the reference to dawn, you will be relieved to hear, may be taken as symbolic) take the seven 'pot-shaped' breaths referred to in the text.

Most people breathe with a movement of the chest and rib-cage: observe your own breathing for a moment and note exactly what happens. 'Pot-breathing' occurs when you take in air by using the abdomen (which, on a full breath, sticks out and grows rounded like a pot). By using the abdoment you take in far more air than usual. On the outbreath, pull the abdomen in so that it becomes concave, a motion which will expel all stagnant air from the lungs. Do not be tempted to try this more than the seven times mentioned, especially if you are unused to breathing exercises, or you may find yourself growing dizzy.

Carry out the elevenfold resolve as instructed in the text, then move on to concentration on the 'dot situated between the eyebrows.' This is, of course, the location of the fabulous Third Eye, associated with the pineal gland, and widely assumed by occultists to be the seat of psychic powers. It is also, although not shown on our diagram, a chakra or energy centre and thus capable of stimulation through visualization. When first visualized, you should see it as a small white sphere, the colour of bone. Once established in your mind's eye, imagine it glowing either red, if you are by nature a calm individual, or green if you are nervous.

Follow this regime for 10 days before moving on to the final stage if results are not forthcoming. Most of the third stage instructions will be clear enough to you by now, since they really only represent more of the same. The important new element is the appearance of the 'black dot' at the base of the generative organs.

This new visualization stimulates the *mudra chakra* which lies between the root of the penis and the anus in a man and between the back of the vagina and the anus in a woman. It is the trigger for very powerful energies indeed and requires to be manipulated with extreme caution. Do *not* visualize this chakra in any colour other than black; and do not visualize it larger than the pill suggested in the text. A small stimulation is quite enough to get results.

6.

Astral Doorways

Lucid dreaming will introduce you to the Astral Plane, but there is no doubt at all that the astral environment in which you find yourself will have been self-created – that is, it will tend to reflect your own unconscious needs, obsessions and desires. This is because however quickly you manage to become aware that you are dreaming, you begin to dream *first*; which means that your environment is created while you are unconscious. Once created, it will tend to retain its form for the remainder of that particular astral adventure. There is always the possibility of non-created elements intruding, of course, but overall the experience will usually tell you far more about yourself than the Other-world.

You already know, from the theoretical sections of this workbook, that there are vast *pre-formed* areas of the Astral Plane, permanent, or semi-permanent, reflections of various energies and influences. It would obviously be very useful to find some sort of doorway into these realms so that you might visit them at will, more or less uncontaminated by the flickering influence of your unconscious mind. (There is a point to be made here, in passing. It seems to me that when you find yourself in what one might call a virgin area of the Astral Plane, such as one does in dreams, the *only* influence on the billows of astral light is your unconscious mind. Consequently, your environment will mirror your personal concerns automatically and continuously. But when you find yourself in an astral district which is *already* reflecting a physical terrain or long-established thought-form, it requires a conscious effort on your part to change your surroundings in any way. Sometimes it requires considerable concentration and skill.)

Doorways into established astral areas actually exist; and have been used by Oriental magicians for centuries. Certain of them were imported into Britain during the Victorian era and the techniques associated with their use distributed to members of the Hermetic Order of the Golden Dawn.

The notion of a doorway into another dimension has been popularized in science fiction where it is usually described as a shimmering portal hanging mysteriously in mid-air through which the hero steps, usually to vanish altogether from the view of mortal men. You will be disappointed to learn that real astral doorways are not a bit like that, although their usage is every bit as fascinating. There is, in this respect, an interesting story about an early meeting between the Irish poet William Butler Yeats and the magician S.L. MacGregor Mathers, who was at the time head of the newly-formed Golden Dawn.

Yeats had heard how Florence Farr, the actress, visited Mathers who placed a square of cardboard on her forehead which instantly triggered a vision of herself walking on a clifftop with screaming seagulls overhead. Yeats too was given a piece of cardboard by Mathers and when he pressed it against his forehead he found himself in the grip of vivid mental images over which he had no control. He was in a desert with a black Titan rising up out of ancient ruins.

In his *Autobiography*, Yeats explained that Mathers told him he had seen a being of the 'Order of Salamanders' because he had been shown their symbol. But Mathers maintained the physical symbol (depicted on card) was not actually necessary – it would have been enough if he had simply imagined it. Yeats was understandably impressed and later joined the Order.

The symbol shown to Florence Farr almost certainly looked like this:

The one placed on Yeats' forehead was:

The colouring of Ms Farr's symbol was blue. Yeats' was red. They were two of a set known as *tattwa* symbols developed by Hindu philosophers, associated with the ancient alchemical elements of earth, air, fire, water and ether and used within the Golden Dawn in a very special way.

Tattwa symbols will, if placed on the forehead as described, frequently trigger the sort of visions Farr and Yeats experienced. But manipulated slightly differently, they become an important aid to astral plane projection. And since they will *direct* the projector to a specific area of the Astral Plane, they are very rightly seen as astral doorways.

The major tattwa symbols look like this:

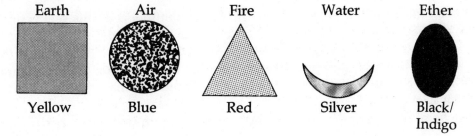

Each one gives access to a specific area of the Astral Plane, but many other elemental doorways may be constructed through the use of *composite* symbols – superimposing the silver crescent of Water on the yellow square of earth, for example, or the red triangle of Fire on the blue disc of air. Experimentation with composite doorways can give intriguing results and you may like to try it at a later date, but for the moment, I propose to stick with the five major elemental doorways since they are a little easier for beginners. The techniques you need to use composite doorways are exactly the same as the one I will be giving for these.

In the Golden Dawn, the tattwas were used as the basis of the Order's earliest experiments in clairvoyance and scrying – the latter term more or less synonymous with what I have called astral plane projection. The theory behind their use was quite complex.

I have already mentioned the universal energy *ch'i* which is usually called *prana* within the schools of Indian yoga. This energy, associated with the air, but distinct from it, is believed to originate in a steady stream from the sun – although it is not of any of the radiations which scientists have yet measured. This radiation has a fivefold aspect, respectively referred to by the Hindus as *akasa* (ether or spirit), *vayu* (air) *tejas* (fire) *apas* (water) and *prithivi* (earth.)

The English translations have little enough to do with the sort of air, fire, water etc that you would recognize, but refer instead to the alchemical elements of those names. Alchemists tried to distinguish between their elements and their more mundane counterparts by using phrases like *air of the wise, fire of the wise* and so on, but this frankly sorted out nobody's confusion. The problem was that while the alchemists spent much time in musty laboratories mixing chemical reagents, their real work – well hidden behind the appalling mass of (sometimes coded) verbiage which comprises the bulk of alchemical literature – was with the basic substance of the Astral Plane.

To understand what this means requires a brief sortie into the world of Qabalah, that body of ancient doctrine which underpins much of modern occultism. Central to the Qabalah was a glyph, which we shall be examining in more detail in a later chapter, called the *Tree of Life*. From one viewpoint, this glyph purports to be a sort of map of reality, showing its ultimate structure as it emerged out of the Great Unmanifest. The glyph has 10 spheres, the bottom-most of which, called *Malkuth*, represents the physical universe. Directly above the Malkuth is a sphere entitled *Yesod*, which represents the Astral Plane. But 'Yesod' does not mean 'Astral Plane' – it means *Foundation*. Because Qabalists – and most other occultists – believe the Astral Plane is the foundation of physical matter.

Given the ease with which the Astral Light is influenced, this seems on the face of it unlikely, but the notion that the astral *underlies* the physical is at the root of most Western magical practice. All rituals and most spells have their inner, astral, aspect; and it is the stresses which these operations set up in the astral which eventually 'earth' themselves to produce 'magical' results on the physical level.

Alchemical experiments were (and are) unusual in that they seek to manipulate and understand two levels simultaneously. The categorization of physical matter into five 'elements' quickly shows the limitations which have persuaded modern scientists to dismiss alchemy as 'proto-chemistry'. But while the art of alchemy certainly gave rise to the science of chemistry, the dismissal indicates a basic lack of understanding. Alchemy is not *proto*-anything, but a workable system in its own right, for the elemental sub-division seems to remain valid for the 'mind-stuff' of the Astral Light.

The force of the elements is not constant within the Astral Light, but follows a sun-driven rhythm. Akasa – ether or spirit – is strongest at dawn when the sun rises and holds its power for two hours when it blends into an ascending *Vayu*, or air. This persists for two hours before blending into *Tejas*, fire, which in turn blends into *Apas*, water, with the cycle finishing in *Prithivi*, earth.

This rhythm of the Universal *prana* or *ch'i* is mirrored by the rhythmic flow of personal *ch'i* within the acupuncture meridians of the human body, which also follows a diurnal rhythm and has its own 'Law of the Five Elements'.

No element actually *replaces* any other in this universal cycle, for *ch'i* is always a mixture of the five. What the cycle signifies is the dominance of a particular element at a given time.

How all this manifests on the Astral Plane is a matter of experience. And to gain that experience, your first job is to make for yourself a set of tattwa cards. Use squares of white cardboard sufficiently large to allow a symbol two to two-and-a-half inches in height. If you decide to make a composite card, this size refers to the *primary* symbol. The secondary symbol, which is superimposed, can – and should – be a little smaller.

Leave the back of the cards plain white and blank. The diagram on page 99 shows you the five primary symbols and the colour associated with each of them. (The symbol for ether should be coloured *either* indigo or black, but not both: and for what it is worth, I have always found indigo works slightly better.) In each case, the colour should be as strong and brilliant as possible. Water colours are quite useless for these cards. Oils are only a little better. Acrylics give the strength and brilliance you need; or you can take the advice contained in the original Golden Dawn documents, which suggested cutting and pasting coloured papers. Certainly foil makes a better silver crescent even than a metallic-based paint.

Composite cards should be made by superimposing a smaller version of the secondary symbol on the primary symbol. As a working example, the tattwa card signifying Fire of Earth would show the primary earth symbol as a yellow square with $2\frac{1}{2}''$ sides, while the red, equilateral fire triangle would have sides about $\frac{1}{2}''$ long. Other composite cards can be made keeping these proportions in mind, although what looks good to the eye should always take precedence over any slavish attempt to duplicate the proportions exactly. More important is clarity and purity of colour, which should be as close to the primaries as possible.

The Golden Dawn instructions suggest writing the appropriate divine and angelic names on the back, but this is purely as an aid to memory and there is good reason for leaving the back of the card blank.

When you have created your symbol cards to your satisfaction, cover them with transparent artist's film or, better still, give them a coat of clear gloss varnish to enhance the colours and preserve the symbols.

There are two ways to use the cards, one of which (holding one to your forehead) you have already learned. This method, in my experience triggers subjective visions – subjective, that is, in the sense that you will perceive them as exercises of the visual imagination. But as we have already seen, even subjectivity is relative and this form of symbol and manipulation is an excellent way of training your imagination to become a periscope which will enable you to *look* into astral levels, even if you are not actually *travelling* there.

The talent is by no means trivial. Developing it was one of the main reasons I was forced to conclude the Astral Plane was essentially objective. When you grow accustomed to obseving the Astral Plane in this way, it is perfectly possible to watch the antics of actual travellers and compare notes afterwards to establish the accuracy of your vision.

At first, there is nothing to distinguish between this form of scrying and normal imagination – indeed, for a long time I assumed the ability was no more than the discovery that imagination itself can peer into astral realms. But eventually you will notice a very subtle difference. This is a lot easier to experience than describe, but essentially astral vision seems to have a greater stability. Until you learn the feel of astral vision, the best way to differentiate is to practise with a partner who has proficiency in the doorways and compare notes.

Use of your cards to trigger projection is a little more complicated. One set of Golden Dawn instructions suggests preliminary meditation on the element you are going to use, saturating yourself with it until, in the case of fire you actually feel hot, in the case of water you feel wet and so on. This is not a bad idea if your main thrust is simply to provide yourself with the most effective route through the doorway. But if you are approaching the experience experimentally, it is probably best to forgo preliminary meditation since it obviously acts as a powerful self-suggestion, thus confusing your results.

The doorway sequence itself is as follows:

Find a quiet room and a comfortable chair. Select your symbol card, sit back and relax as deeply as possible. Gaze intently at the coloured symbol for about half a minute, then turn the card over and gaze at its blank back. As you do so, an optical reflex will cause the symbol you have been studying to appear on the back of the card. The process is quite automatic, so there is no need for you to try to force or will it – simply wait a second or two and it will happen.

The symbol itself will be quite clearly defined, but in the direct complementary colour to the original and oddly luminescent. The yellow earth square, for example, would appear as lavender or mauve, depending on the exact shade of yellow used. (There is no need, incidentally, to use the back of the card if you do not want to. A sheet of white paper will do just as well, as will a blank wall or even the ceiling. But the card back is very convenient and if you *do* decide, to use something else, make sure the surface is white and not cream or any other colour, otherwise the tones will be slightly off.)

Once you have seen your complementary-coloured symbol, close your eyes and interiorize it. What you are trying to do is visualize what you have just seen, but the visualization works best if you imagine yourself *drawing in* the glowing symbol until it is established inside your head. At this point, you should mentally enlarge the symbol until it is big enough for you to pass through. Then imagine yourself stepping through the enlarged symbol as if it were an actual door.

People differ considerably in their ability to take this step, although I have yet to meet anyone who could not manage it eventually with practice.

In the Golden Dawn, students were encouraged to use the Sign of the Enterer, a 'groping for the light' which I stated erroneously in *Astral Doorways* to be more or less identical to the straight-armed Nazi salute. In fact, this sign uses *both* hands and has a projective influence. You are instructed to take a small, sliding step forward, while simultaneously raising both arms above your head. As you complete the step, bring your hands over your head forwards and thrust them out horizontally, fingers out, palms downwards, at the level of your eyes. Sink your head until your eyes are looking out directly between your thumbs.

If you can get the hang of all this, you are instructed to stand up, still visualizing the enlarged doorway, make the sign physically and simultaneously imagine yourself moving through, then take your seat again and continue with the vision.

Once you have reached this stage, you should strongly imagine the doorway *behind* you, hanging luminous in the air like one of those science fiction doorways we mentioned earlier. Then look around and take note of your surroundings. At this point, if you were a member of the Golden Dawn, you would be urged to vibrate the Divine Names associated with the element you had chosen.

This is a difficult area for anyone who has not been trained in Qabalah. Briefly, certain entities, ranked all the way from deities to elementals, are believed to be associated with particular astral areas. From one viewpoint, the use of their names is similar to religious supplication or prayer – a calling on their aid in your endeavours. From a slightly different viewpoint, the use of their names is a courtesy, a greeting to the more important inhabitants of a country you are about to enter.

But the names are to be *vibrated* – i.e. pronounced in a special way – which suggests they may be more in the nature of a password or, even more correctly, a direct manipulation of the essence of the plane in its particular elemental aspect. Their effect is to make the experience more vivid and (according to Golden Dawn theory) safer. Whether you wish to use the names at this point is a personal decision – certainly it is perfectly possible to carry through an elemental projection without them. But assuming that you *do* propose to use them, a little practice in vibration is recommended.

Magical vibration of a name is a technique by which it is half chanted back in the throat in such a way that it *buzzes*, thus creating a literal and physical vibration which can be felt quite clearly by yourself and by anyone else who happened to be nearby. Vibration is an art in itself. With practice you can persuade it to trigger almost anywhere within your own body or outside it, like a ventriloquist throwing his voice. For the purpose of the present exercise, however, it will be enough to practise until you have achieved the distinctive buzzing pronunciation of the names.

The names themselves are Hebrew and are spelled out phonetically for you in the table below. The pronunciation is somewhat different in magical usage to normal usage, so please stick with the pronunciation given. All names should be vibrated slowly and audibly.

The recommended sequence is 1) Deity Name, three to four times; 2) Archangelic Name; 3) Angelic Name; 4) Element Name; 5) Cardinal Quarter Name. The full table is as follows:

Earth
Deity Name: *Ah-doh-nay hah-Ahr-retz*
Archangelic Name: *Or-eee-ell*
Angelic Name: *Four-lack*
Element Name: *Oh-fire*
Cardinal Name: *Zah-fawn*

Air
Deity Name: *Shah-day ell chay*
Archangelic Name: *Rah-fai-ell*
Angelic Name: *Cha-san*
Element Name: *Rue-ach*
Cardinal Name: *Miz-rack*

Water
Deity Name: *Aye-low-eem Zah-bah-oth*
Archangelic Name: *Gah-brah-ell*
Angelic Name: *Tah-lee-ah-had*
Element Name: *Maim*
Cardinal Name: *Mah-rab*

Fire
Deity Name: *Yod-heh-vav-heh Zah-bah-oth*
Archangelic Name: *Me-kay-ell*
Angelic Name: *Ah-ral*
Element Name: *Ash*
Cardinal Name: *Dah-rom*

Once you have used these names, Golden Dawn teaching suggests that:

'Various changes may now be perceived to occur in the landscape; it will become alive, vivified and dynamic and the sense of the element should become even more clearly and vividly defined.

Also, a being may appear, one whose characteristics pertain to the Element, and his garments, their colours, and his other ornaments should be in the appropriate colours.

'Under *no* circumstances should the Seer wander from his doorway alone: he should always wait until one of these elemental beings or 'guides' appears and he should continue vibrating the names until one does appear, or until he obtains the sense that one is present.

'Sometimes, and with some students, there is no clear vision of these occurrences or beings, but only a sense of intuition or powerful instinct that such and such a thing is happening, and that such a type of being has appeared. This often is more trustworthy than the use of sight or other sense.'

Weird though it sounds, my own experience indicates all of this is excellent advice, although I do have to admit to various uneventful trips without the aid of a guide. If, when you have experience of the Astral Plane, you decide to go solo, remember to make a careful note of the road you are travelling, since you will obviously want to return to the doorway to get back to the physical world.

Golden Dawn magicians, who were extremely cautious individuals, would typically test any guide who appeared by giving the sign of the grade appropriate to the element visited. (For earth, this was the Zelator Sign, which really *is* identical to the Nazi salute.) They would then decide on his *bona fides* depending on what sign he gave back. I am an extremely cautious individual myself, but the exchange of signs is meaningless to anyone outside a magical Order – and even within an Order, the signs have to be related to one's own training. In the absence of formal training, therefore, I can only suggest you judge astral guides in exactly the same way you judge physical plane acquaintances – by their appearance and actions. There is no need to become paranoid: the Astral Plane is no more dangerous than the physical, although there is certainly a tendency to attract entities which are sympathetic to your personality characteristics.

7.

The Astral I Ching

While driving to work in a slow-moving line of traffic several years ago. I saw an approaching lorry swing abruptly onto the wrong side of the road. There was the sound of a collision somewhere ahead and the line of traffic stopped at once. I got out of my vehicle and ran forward to find the lorry had struck a Mini car. The driver, a heavily pregnant woman, and her companion, another woman, were both shocked but unhurt. I ran to the driver of the lorry, who was bent over the steering wheel, and asked if he was all right. He too seemed shocked and told me vaguely he had bruised his wrist. At this point, it appeared to be one of the less serious road accidents with no bad injuries and minimal damage to either vehicle. But then I walked past the lorry and discovered a second Mini. Two of its occupants were already dead. The third died in an ambulance on the way to hospital.

I felt compelled to inflict this little horror story on you because of something which had happened earlier that morning. Some time before eight a.m. when I left for work, I consulted an oracle and required it to give me an indication of the influences on the day ahead. *He shall see a wagon full of corpses,* the oracle replied.

If this was coincidence, it was the sort of coincidence which had occurred far too often in the past and was to occur again far too often in the future. Each morning for more than two years, I consulted the oracle with exactly the same question: *What are the influences on the coming day?* Each evening, I reviewed the day and attempted to determine how far, if at all, the pronouncements I received matched what had actually happened. Over and over again, I discovered they matched uncannily well, especially after regular practice enabled me to determine exactly what some of the more obscure pronouncements actually meant.

I was not the only one to be impressed. The psychiatrist Carl Jung once experimented with the same oracle and decided that had it been human, he would have been forced, on the basis of the answers he received, to pronounce it of sound mind. The oracle we used was Chinese *I Ching,* claimed to be the oldest book in the world . . . and possibly the wisest.

The principle of the *I Ching,* the subdivision of phenomena into negative and positive forces called *yin* and *yang,* was an aspect of Chinese thought dating from the furthest reaches of prehistory. Technically, the oracle professes to read

The I Ching Hexagrams

䷀ Creative	䷁ Receptive	䷂ Difficulty at Beginning	䷃ Youthful Folly
䷄ Waiting for Nourishment	䷅ Conflict	䷆ The Army	䷇ Holding Together
䷈ Taming Power of the Small	䷉ Treading	䷊ Peace	䷋ Standstill
䷌ Fellowship with Men	䷍ Possession in Great measure	䷎ Modesty	䷏ Enthusiasm
䷐ Following	䷑ Work on what has been spoiled	䷒ Approach	䷓ Contemplation
䷔ Biting Through	䷕ Grace	䷖ Splitting Apart	䷗ Turning Point
䷘ Unexpected	䷙ Taming Power of the Great	䷚ Providing Nourishment	䷛ Preponderance of the Great
䷜ Abysmal	䷝ Clinging Fire	䷞ Influence	䷟ Duration
䷠ Retreat	䷡ Power of the Great	䷢ Progress	䷣ Darkening of the Light
䷤ The Family	䷥ Opposition	䷦ Obstruction	䷧ Deliverance
䷨ Decrease	䷩ Increase	䷪ Breakthrough	䷫ Coming to Meet
䷬ Gathering Together	䷭ Pushing Upward	䷮ Exhaustion	䷯ The Well
䷰ Revolution	䷱ The Cauldron	䷲ The Arousing	䷳ Keeping Still
䷴ Gradual Progress	䷵ Marrying Maiden	䷶ Abundance	䷷ The Wanderer
䷸ The Gentle	䷹ The Joyous	䷺ Dispersion	䷻ Limitation
䷼ Inner Truth	䷽ Preponderance of the Small	䷾ After Completion	䷿ Before Completion

the current state of *yin* and *yang* through the development of six-lined figures known as *hexagrams*. The hexagrams themselves have a long, if somewhat disreputable, history in that they sprang from a very ancient form of fortune-telling in which tortoise shells were heated until they cracked and the patterns interpreted by experts. In time, so our own historical experts insist, the cracks became stylized into three-lined figures (trigrams featuring broken (yin) and unbroken (yang) lines.

Some time prior to 1150 B.C., a provincial noble named Wen proved virtue is not its own reward by behaving in such an upright, honourable and decent way that the Emperor had him thrown into prison. The problem was Wen's popularity, which the Emperor (correctly) believed outshone his own.

With nothing better to do to fill his days, Wen turned to intellectual pursuits and began to assign definitive meanings to the trigrams which were already in use as fortune-telling devices. He combined them into the six-lined hexagrams and added his own brief commentary, called a Judgement, to each.

The Emperor eventually released him and Wen showed his gratitude by leading a rebellion which overthrew the dynasty. Wen himself died before he could seize the throne, but scholars have awarded him the posthumous title of King. Wen's son, the Duke of Chou, consolidated the victory and finished his father's work, adding his own commentaries on the individual lines. The completed work became known as the *Changes of Chou (Chou I)* or, more simply, the *Book of Changes* (a literal translation of *I Ching*.) By this time, it had totally outgrown the early crudities of fortune-telling and become a tome of profound philosophy, masquerading as a system of divination. At a later stage, Confucius, who was already an old man when he came upon the *I Ching*, added further commentaries and explanations.

There are, in the *I Ching*, 64 hexagrams, shown with their titles on page 107 Not only is each hexagram capable of interpretation, but each *line* of each hexagram is also capable of interpretation. Lines are, however, only interpreted when it is thought they contain such tension that they are about to change into their opposites. Once they do so, they produce a new hexagram which is interpreted in context with the original.

This sounds complicated if you are unfamiliar with the system, but only means that the oracle is capable of delivering more than four thousand answers without repeating itself. You can get an idea of the sort of answer it delivers from this example.

Ting/The Cauldron
above Li The Clinging, Fire
below Sun The Gentle, Wind, Wood

The Judgement
The Cauldron. Supreme good fortune.
Success.

The Image
Fire over wood.
The images of The Cauldron.
Thus the superior man consolidates his fate
By making his position correct.

The Lines
Six at the beginning means:
A *ting* with legs upturned.
Furthers removal of stagnating stuff.
One takes a concubine for the sake of her son.
No blame.

Nine in the second place means:
There is food in the *ting*.
My comrades are envious.
But they cannot harm me.
Good fortune.

Nine in the third place means:
The handle of the *ting* is altered.
One is impeded in his way of life.
The fat of the pheasant is not eaten.
Once rain falls, remorse is spent.
Good fortune comes in the end.

Nine in the fourth place means:
The legs of the *ting* are broken.
The prince's meal is spilled
And his person is soiled.
Misfortune.

Six in the fifth place means:
The *ting* has yellow handles, golden carrying rings.
Perserverence furthers.

Nine at the top means:
The *ting* has rings of jade.
Great good fortune.
Nothing that would not act to further.

   This is not the most accessible of answers. But in quoting it (from the Baynes translation published by Routledge & Kegan Paul) I decided not to trouble you with the extensive commentaries which make it a little easier to understand.
   Those curious phrases under the heading *Lines* – 'Six at the beginning . . . ', 'Nine in the second place . . . ' and so on – refer to the way a hexagram is built

up during a consultation. This is quite easily done using three coins. You can still buy reproductions of the sort of antique Chinese coins (with a hole in the middle) traditionally used to consult the *I Ching*, but modern coins of any country work perfectly well. Decide which is the front and which the back, if this is not already obvious, then toss all three simultaneously and note how they fall.

The front side of each coin counts as a *yin* with a value of 2. The reverse is a *yang* with a value of 3. This produces the following values for any given toss of the coins:

All heads or fronts (*yin + yin + yin*) = 6
All tails or reverse sides (*yang + yang + yang*) = 9
Two heads, one tail (*yin + yin + yang*) =7
Two tails, one head (*yang + yang + yin*) = 8

Your first toss of the coins gives you the bottom line of your hexagram. If you scored an 8 (two tails and a head) the line is known as a *young yin* and shown as

— —

If you scored a 7 (two heads, one tail) the line is a *young yang* shown as

——

If you scored a 9 (all tails) the line is known as an *old yang* and is shown as

—o—

If you scored a 6 (all heads) the line becomes an *old yin* and is shown as

—x—

Toss the coins again to find the next line up of your hexagram – hexagrams are always built from the bottom upwards – and keep going for a total of six tosses until you have the whole figure. *Old yins* and *old yangs* are the lines I mentioned earlier which have the property of reversing themselves (*yin* into *yang*, *yang* into *yin*). If any appear in your hexagram, reverse them and draw a second figure beside the first. If, for example, your first figure looked like this . . .

. . . it would change into this hexagram . . .

. . . and you would write the whole thing like this:

Six at the top
Six in the third place   Changes to:
Nine in the first place

If you do not already own a copy of the *I Ching*, this may sound like a lot of work to no real purpose, since you cannot even ask the oracle a question and get a proper answer. But it is not, in fact, quite true to say this, for proper answers *are* possible without recourse to any of the traditional interpretations at all. This is due to the fact that, unsuspected by a majority of its users, the *I Ching* is an astral machine. The oracle has two astral aspects, the first of which arises during a ritual consultation.

Ritual consultations of the *I Ching* are quite complex. To undertake one, you will require your three coins, a box to keep them in, a silk cloth, a black divining cloth, incense and burner, paper and pen or pencil, a bowl of water and a towel. You would also normally need a copy of the *I Ching* itself, but since, in this instance, you are edging towards an astral operation, you can substitute a copy of the hexagrams and their titles shown on page 107. Draw these out carefully and write the titles beside them on good quality paper or card.

The copy of the *I Ching* or your copy of the hexagrams should be wrapped in the silk cloth and stored on a shelf above shoulder height until you begin your ritual consultation. Either one is the 'earthing point' for certain activities going on in the Astral Plane.

Before you start, polish your three coins until they are bright and shining, then boil them in salted water to leave them free of any subtle energy impressions. Keep them in a special box you have bought or made for the purpose. This box, like everything else associated with the rituals, should not be used for any other purpose; nor should any item – and especially the coins – be handled by anyone other than yourself.

Begin the ritual in a quiet room where you are unlikely to be disturbed. Sit or kneel facing south (if you are in the northern hemisphere: otherwise face north) and spread your black divination cloth on the table or floor before you. Lay the book (or your copy of the hexagrams) in front of you at the far side of the cloth. Take time to go through a process of conscious relaxation until you are completely calm. Wash your hands in the bowl of water and dry them with the towel. Now begin to visualize a figure standing just beyond the book.

The figure should be imagined as a slim, robed Chinese male, very old, with a wisp of white beard. He is a little over average height, dressed in white robes and holds a rolled scroll in one hand.

The technique of visualization is very similar to the Body of Light technique you practised earlier, except that you are not, of course, creating any sort of projection vehicle. The figure you establish is, in fact, an astral shell suitable for the spirit of the *I Ching*. This spirit actually exists, inhabiting a level *beyond* the Astral Plane. It is linked in ways I do not pretend to understand with the hexagrams. This linkage means, in part, that if you create a suitable astral vehicle – that is, if you visualize the figure properly – the spirit will, so to speak, come down to animate it.

Given practice, the visualization will produce something very similar to Madame David-Neel's *tulpa*, except that in the clearly-defined circumstances of the ritual, there is little possibility of it changing its nature or wandering away. But it will – right from the start if you do a good job – be completely independent of your mind, even while the visualization is still internal. You may find this a little weird at first, although the process is very similar to the way fictional characters break free of their authors.

Once you have established the Chinese sage, you should *kow-tow* three times towards him, knocking your forehead against the floor or table-top. Although this is no more than a mark of respect, you may, as a product of a Western culture, find it demeaning, in which case you should substitute whatever other mark of respect you believe to be more appropriate.

With the astral figure in place, ask your question aloud, then write it down on a piece of paper to 'earth' it. Take your three coins from the special box, light the incense burner and pass the coins clockwise through the smoke. When you have done so, shake them in your cupped hands while concentrating on the question, then throw them on your divination cloth to build up your hexagram in the way previously given.

Draw your hexagram on a separate sheet of paper, one line at a time. If the completed figure contains any *old yin* or *old yang* lines, change them to their opposite and draw a second hexagram beside the first. Check the title of the hexagram(s) from the list on page 107 and write that down too.

At this point, if you are working with a full *I Ching* text, you can consult the Wen/Chou/Confucius interpretations. But if not, or if you can make no sense out of the interpretations, you can consult the spirit of the *I Ching* directly. Simply ask the astral figure to explain the meaning of the answer and listen (mentally) to his answer. Finally, it is always a good idea to write the explanation down.

Consulting the *I Ching* in this way is an operation of astral magic which, if you have a talent for it, brings far more detailed and interesting results than the more conventional approach. But it is not the only astral operation you can carry out with the *I Ching*. The hexagrams themselves may actually be used as astral doorways.

The technique employed is a little similar to that used to open the *tattwa* doorways, but does not involve any optical reflex or complementary colours. While you are seated quietly and totally relaxed in a place where you will not be disturbed, visualize your chosen hexagram on a stout, closed, wooden door. Work on this until you can see it clearly in your mind's eye, then continue to observe the door and wait. After a time the door will swing open of its own accord, at which point you should imagine yourself rising from your chair and walking through the doorway. Once through, you should take care to imagine the door *behind* you, exactly as you did with the *tattwa* doors. And here again, you should take careful note of where you go within the astral environment so that you can find your way back whenever you wish.

There is nothing to stop you selecting a hexagram at random in order to practise this sort of projection, but you will find it a far more satisfying – and potentially a more useful – experience, if you first engage on a full, ritual consultation of the oracle exactly as outlined earlier.

In this instance, once you have drawn your hexagram, visualize it on the door as before. You will find that the Chinese sage will then open the door and will often accompany you through. The answer to your question will be contained in your experiences after you pass through the doorway. If there were moving lines in your original hexagram, it is possible to visualize both the original and the second hexagrams on the door side by side, or you can undertake two sequential astral trips using first and second hexagrams respectively.

8.

Working the Qabalistic Tree

At twenty past eight on the morning of Sunday, 1 June, 1930, Violet Firth sat down to begin a fascinating occult experiment. Better known by her pseudonym, Dion Fortune, she was a trained Initiate of the Golden Dawn and a founder of her own magical Order, the Society of the Inner Light. Thus she seated herself in an Egyptian godform position facing south-east and rapidly drew an astral circle.

As a natural psychic, she was aware not only of her subtle bodies, but of a small, semi-permanent kink in the silver cord which attached etheric and physical. She turned quickly to the north-east to smooth this out, then projected her astral body to the centre of the circle.

Although the only extant account of her experiment takes great care to avoid any technical information (which was still secret when the account was first published in 1932) it seems likely that she used some variation of the Body of Light technique to trigger the projection. In all probability, she was sufficiently experienced for any formulation of the Body of Light to call out her own astral body automatically.

She turned the phantom to face east, the direction of the rising sun, and invoked the God names of the middle Pillar, an exercise designed to energize five major chakras located along the centre of the body. These names are (phonetically) *Yeck-id-ah Eh-heh-yeh, Yeh-hoh-voh Eh-loh-eem, Yeh-hoh-voh El-oh-ah vey-Da-as, Shah-day El-cahy,* and *Ah-doh-nay hah-arh-retz.**
When they are vibrated during an out-of-body experience, they cause a dramatic strengthening of the astral vehicle. Dion Fortune reported, 'Clear projection. Consciousness very definitely centred in astral body.'

At this point, she 'formulated a path to a certain astral temple.' Every magical organization that goes beyond empty ritual has its own linked temple on the Astral Plane and carefully constructed ways to reach it. Dion Fortune would have been familiar with the astral temples of both the Golden Dawn and her own esoteric organization, but in this instance, the temple she referred to was the Qabalistic Temple of Malkuth, frequently used by magicians with a Qabalistic background.

*For a full exposition of this exercise see *The Middle Pillar* by Israel Regardie.

In the robing room, she put on a white robe and a striped head-dress, passed through a bright, cheery astral environment, then entered the temple where she sat down, facing east, on a large stone block. By now she had lost all sense of her physical body. To understand what happened next requires a little knowledge of Qabalah.

Tree of Life

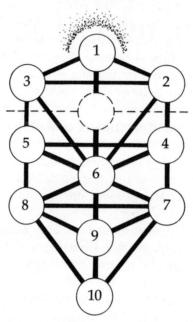

Take a close look at the diagram. It shows the central glyph of modern, esoteric Qabalism – the Tree of Life. To Qabalists, it is a diagram of reality, showing the relationships between various of its major aspects. The 10 numbered circles, known as *Sephiroth* (singular: *Sephirah*) are usually perceived as energies or states on the physical level, but exist as defined *places* on the Astral Plane. So, as we shall see later, do the tracks between them.

While Dion Fortune sat on the stone block, her astral body (which she had previously noted was full of vitality) began to rise upwards. She allowed it to rise until it passed through the roof of the building and into bright sunlight. It continued to rise rapidly until it passed beyond a layer of cloud so that she looked down on the bright, sunlit, cotton wool floor so familiar to air travellers. The sky itself began to darken to indigo and she saw a very large, bright crescent moon. 'I knew,' she noted afterwards, 'I was entering the sphere of Yesod.'

Malkuth, where the temple was, is marked as sphere 10 on the diagram. Yesod, marked 9, is immediately above it. It is the sphere most intimately associated with the Astral Plane itself and, as such, one of its major symbols is the moon. By entering the Temple of Malkuth, then proceeding directly upwards, Dion Fortune was making good use of her occult training. She was, in effect, using the Tree of Life not exactly as a doorway, but as a map of astral territory. Once she found herself in one known district of the map – as she did when she entered Malkuth – she could use the glyph to find her way to others.

She decided her trip was going well. Further above her, she saw the sun of Tiphareth (numbered 6 on the diagram) set in an area of golden sky, but looking more like a theatrical backdrop than a real sun. 'Continued to rise to the Central Pillar,' she wrote, 'with no sense of strain but a feeling of breathless rapidity, wondering where I was going next.'

It did not take her long to decide that where she was going next was Kether, the topmost sphere of the Tree, numbered 1 on the diagram, symbol of unity and godhead. En route, she 'passed through a sphere in which I saw shadowy angel forms with the traditional harps sitting on clouds all around me.' This sphere, it seems certain, was Daath, which is not actually numbered on our diagram because Qabalists believe that while intimately associated with the Tree, it exists in a different dimension. It is shown astride a dotted line marking the area of the abyss, the demarcation zone between the rarefied Supernals – topmost three Sephiroth – and the remainder of the Tree.

With all this talk of glyphs and symbols, it is tempting to think of Dion Fortune's experience as inward and personal, but while there were undoubtedly personal elements in her perceptions, the overall journey was entirely objective, a 'Rising on the Planes', the details of which a traveller with no Qabalistic knowledge confirmed for me several years ago. In this context, my traveller also found the angels of the Daath sphere difficult to see clearly, but remained long enough to describe them as powerful, uni-directional and (emotionally) cold.

Still rising, Dion Fortune entered a sphere of blinding white light, which she believed to be Kether (1 on the diagram). As she had earlier lost touch with her physical body, she now found she could no longer sense even her astral vehicle. She had become a point of consciousness without qualities, retaining her individuality only as a single spark of essential life. She had an awareness of the veils of Negative Existence behind Kether 'as the darkness of a starless night, stretching to infinity.' (This last reference is to an area of Qabalistic doctrine which resembles the Hindu 'Breath of Brahma' theories. According to this doctrine, the universe existed in unmanifest form before coming into being; and will eventually return to unmanifest form as part of an eternal cycle. Qabalists symbolize the unmanifest 'background' of the universe by means of three veils known as the *Ain*, Negativity, *Ain Soph*, the Limitless and *Ain Soph Aur*, Limitless Light.)

Suddenly, in this state of Light, Dion Fortune was turned about, so that her back was, so to speak, towards the Tree. She found herself backed into it . . . and changed. She had become a towering cosmic figure, nude, hermaphrodite and powerful. This figure was the full size of the Tree, its feet planted on the bluish Earth sphere, the Supernal Sephiroth about its head. She felt, so she admitted later, like a great angelic being, rising through the entire cosmos, not merely the solar system, against a swelling undertone of music.

The experience ended and she was reabsorbed into the Malkuth sphere, dropping through the roof to find herself seated, normal sized, on the stone block. But the towering figure remained, overshadowing the temple, and she had now developed a bizarre double consciousness: she was aware of herself in the great figure and simultaneously in the smaller figure in the temple.

At that point, there was a mundane interruption. Dogs began to bark and children were shouting in the (physical) street outside her window. The Dion Fortune within the smaller figure ordered the larger figure to stop the noise in the street. And the Dion Fortune within the larger figure stretched out her hand over the youngsters making the noise . . . but without any noticeable result.

Her occult training came again to her rescue and she used a mystic sign instead. Her published account blanks out the actual sign, but it was probably no more than the Sign of Harpocrates, the Sign of Silence learned in the Golden Dawn. Whatever the sign, it worked and the noise ceased. 'Consciousness now centred again in the large figure,' wrote Dion Fortune. 'I did not know quite what to do with it as I had never expected such a manifestation and did not know its possibilities.'

Eventually she decided to try projecting energy from the towering figure and this she did very successfully in the form of a down-pouring of golden light. It rushed like water from a hydrant, full of diamond sparkles, first from the palms of her hands, then from the solar plexus and finally from her forehead as well. The altar of the Malkuth temple transformed itself into a hollow stone tank to receive the energy, which ceased to flow as the tank filled.

Dion Fortune felt strongly that the experiment was over and made haste to return to her physical body. She noted that her breathing was very slow and shallow and waited for it to become normal before re-entering the physical. When she did so, she earthed herself with yet another mystic sign and a strong stamp of the foot. The time was 8.45 a.m.

This is a remarkable experience by any standards, even allowing for the fact that Dion Fortune was a natural psychic and highly-trained occultist, and it indicates one way in which the Qabalistic Tree can be used to considerable

Tree and Paths

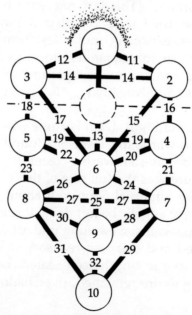

effect. It is not, however, the way it is normally used by Qabalists interested in astral projection. What happens far more often is that the traveller will *walk the paths.*

There are 22 paths on the Tree of Life. If you refer to our diagram, you can actually count them – they are the lines joining the Sephiroth. Each path is a specific astral track and leads to a Sephirah just as surely as Dion Fortune's technique of Rising on the Planes. The doorway into each path is a Tarot trump.

Chances are I do not need to explain the Tarot to you. It is a special 78 card deck which can be used for gaming, but is more often put to fortune-telling. Alongside the 56 suit cards are 22 trumps, very curious pictorial cards long thought to be repositories of arcane symbolism. In modern Qabalah, each trump is associated with a Tree Path.

The various paths of the tree are numbered in the diagram above. The associated trumps are shown in this table:

Path	From	No.	To	No.	Trump
32	Malkuth	10	Yesod	9	The World
31	Malkuth	10	Hod	8	Judgement
30	Yesod	9	Hod	8	The Sun
29	Malkuth	10	Netzach	7	The Moon
28	Yesod	9	Netzach	7	The Emperor
27	Hod	8	Netzach	7	Lightning-struck Tower
26	Hod	8	Tiphareth	6	The Devil
25	Yesod	9	Tiphareth	6	Temperance
24	Netzach	7	Tiphareth	6	Death
23	Hod	8	Geburah	5	The Hanged Man
22	Tiphareth	6	Geburah	5	Justice
21	Netzach	7	Chesed	4	The Wheel of Fortune
20	Tiphareth	6	Chesed	4	The Hermit
19	Geburah	5	Chesed	4	Strength
18	Geburah	5	Binah	3	The Chariot
17	Tiphareth	6	Binah	3	The Lovers
16	Chesed	4	Chokmah	2	The Hierophant
15	Tiphareth	6	Chokmah	2	The Star
14	Binah	3	Chokmah	2	The Empress
13	Tiphareth	6	Kether	1	The High Priestess
12	Binah	3	Kether	1	The Magician
11	Chokmah	2	Kether	1	The Fool

To walk the Paths, you will obviously need a Tarot deck, or at least a full set of Tarot trumps. There are a great many Tarot decks on the market now and more seem to be published every day. For divination, you can use any deck that suits you, since the variation in symbolism has the positive effect of triggering psychism in different people. But for astral work, I would strongly recommend the Marseilles Tarot. This deck is graphically crude and lacks the detailed symbolism of many others – which is why it is so useful for this work: your mind tends to fill in the missing links.

I do not think I would suggest you work the tree fully – that is, walk each path – unless you have had Qabalistic training. But there is no reason why you should not try one of the lower paths as an experiment. In *Astral Doorways*, I gave brief instructions for entering the thirty-second path, linking Malkuth to Yesod. It was selected because its central experience is self-knowledge – an excellent starting point for anyone interested in astral Qabalah. The thirty-first path, Malkuth to Hod, is also quite suited to beginners. It brings insight into your relationships with others and indicates what they can teach you.

The method which follows is in the nature of a visual meditation with no attempt made to project the astral body (as, for example, Dion Fortune did in the experiment described earlier). All the same, you may find a full projection follows on automatically – especially if you have been using any of the techniques given earlier in the workbook.

Like all Qabalistic Paths, the thirty-first has clearly defined symbolism, almost all of it centred around the element of fire. If you find different elemental symbolism creeping into your experience, the chances are that you have wandered off the path and need to backtrack.

You will meet with two great archetypal figures on this exercise – the Archangel Sandalphon, who will help you leave the sphere of Malkuth, and the Archangel Michael, who will greet you when you reach the sphere of Hod. Roughly midway, you are quite likely to come across some representation of the Hebrew letter associated with the path. It is called *shin*, which means 'tooth' and looks like this

The fire symbolism is fairly evident from its appearance.

With the two Archangels and the Hebrew symbol firmly in mind, you have the beginning, middle and end of the path, so you are unlikely to go too far astray. Before you begin, you will need a small table, a lighted candle and, as always, that quiet room where you will not be disturbed. The first stage is to make contact with that Temple of Malkuth from which Dion Fortune began her remarkable journey. Although the technique is internal, the result should be objective. The Temple itself has been burned into the Astral Light by the efforts of thousands of trained Qabalists over hundreds of years and has permanence and stability in its own right. Your visualizations create a linkage which ensures that, at very least, you are observing the astral and, at best, are drawn into it completely. This is what you do:

Set up your candle securely on the table before you to the east, sit comfortably and go through a conscious relaxation process. When you are totally relaxed, look towards the candle flame and allow it to hold your attention. Relax even more deeply and imagine that the room around you is slowly changing. The walls are being replaced by colonnades of strong, black, marble pillars, flecked with gold and highly polished. When you can see these pillars clearly in your mind's eye, turn your attention to the floor, which is also changing to become a black and white chequer-board of inlaid marble, like the floor of a Masonic Temple.

At this point you should close your eyes and absorb the after-image of the candle into your vision. See it now flickering above the black draped double-cube altar which has replaced the table. Allow the flame to grow (much as you did with the *tattwa* symbols when they transformed into doorways) and move towards it until you can see standing within the flame a giant figure, growing steadily until it towers above you, reaching almost to the roof.

The figure is robed in a mixture of olive, citrine, russet and black – the autumn colours of nature. Take time to allow the figure to solidify, for this is Sandalphon, Archangel of the Sphere of Earth and Guardian of the Temple of Malkuth. Beyond the Archangel and the altar, to the east, you can now clearly see three doors, each one covered by a tapestry curtain, each curtain depicting a huge representation of a Tarot trump.

On the central door, you can see the oval of a massive laurel wreath, intertwined with lilies and roses and surrounded (anti-clockwise, from bottom left) by the elemental symbols of a bull, a lion, an eagle and a man, one to each corner. Within the oval, pale in the indigo darkness is an hermaphroditic figure, naked but for a wisp of veil which drapes across its body and carrying a golden spiral in one hand, a silver spiral in the other. This is the Tarot trump number 21, the World or Universe.

On the door to your right, the curtain depicts a very different scene. Two dogs stand baying on a river bank, while from the water crawls a giant lobster, its claws almost touching a scrap of parchment on which is written the syllable *MA*. Beyond the dogs, in the background, rise two stone-built towers. Above them, dominating the scene is a full moon, low to the horizon. This is Tarot trump number 18, the Moon.

The third doorway, to your left, bears the following representation:

This is Tarot trump number 20, the Judgement or Last Judgement and as you absorb its symbolism, Sandalphon moves eastwards from the altar towards it, indicating with a gesture that you may pass through it.

Imagine clearly that you rise from your chair (which has now transformed into the stone block on which Dion Fortune sat) and move towards this doorway. Part the curtain and step through. Your trip has begun.

9.

Guided Tours

All the doorways so far described have been visual – and many more visual doorways certainly exist. But the Hermetic Lodges long ago developed a different technique designed not so much for astral exploration as astral instruction. This was the technique of a *guided pathworking* in which participants joined an experienced magician/guide to walk a very clearly-defined area of the astral and take part in *pre-planned* experiences.

Such workings served a variety of purposes, from initiation to the channelling of power. Some took advantage of the sort of visual symbols you have been using, but many others did not. Instead, very detailed *verbal* instructions were used to paint pictures in the mind. It was believed, with some justification, that such beginnings were closer to the reality of the astral experience than even the best constructed graphic symbol.

Verbal doorways remained the exclusive prerogative of initiate occultists until the early 1980s when the British ritualist, Dolores Ashcroft-Nowicki, decided to go public with the technique. Dolores Ashcroft-Nowicki was an Initiate of Dion Fortune's Society of the Inner Light and a disciple of that remarkable magician W. E. Butler who, with Gareth Knight, founded the highly-respected Servants of the Light School of Occult Science. After Mr Butler's death, Dolores Ashcroft-Nowicki became, on his express instruction, head of the SOL organization and remains so to this day.

Despite these impressive credentials, her decision to unveil details of the guided pathworking techniques outside the esoteric Lodge rooms created a furore among her fellow-occultists, many of whom disapproved deeply of what she was doing. But she felt the time was right for the method to reach a wider audience and persevered with her controversial approach. From public expositions of pathworkings before large, but necessarily limited, audiences, Dolores Ashcroft-Nowicki went into print to reach a larger public.

Her first book on the subject was *The Shining Paths*, a collection of verbal pathworkings centred on the Qabalistic Tree of Life. The work was published by the Aquarian Press in 1983. Four years later, she was in print again with *Highways of the Mind*, an even more detailed exposition of the art and one which contains a fascinating history of its development.

Dolores Ashcroft-Nowicki continued to expand her sphere of influence with a marriage of ancient techniques and modern technology. In 1988 she launched the first of a series of *Invitation to Magic* video tapes designed to bring esoteric methodology into the homes of students via their television sets. The first tape produced was *An Introduction to the Western Mystery Tradition.* Perhaps predictably, it contained, amongst much other material, a full-scale guided pathworking run by Dolores herself.

Although the ideal is obviously the physical presence of an experienced teacher, the use of video is a very close substitute. But if you do not have a copy, you can still experience the use of a verbal doorway by constructing one yourself. For this you will need no more than a tape recorder and a little time.

Prepare your doorway by recording, verbatim, the script which follows. It is taken directly from Dolores Ashcroft-Nowicki's *Introduction to the Western Mystery Tradition* and represents one element out of the total pathworking included in her video. However interesting you find the experience, I would suggest you do not use your recording more than once or twice, otherwise you run the danger of unbalanced results.

Take the trouble to record the script correctly. If you stumble over words or find the overall flow interrupted for any reason, go back and do it again. Try to use emphasis and inflection to create as visual an impression as possible. This is your script:

Make yourself comfortable and start relaxing your body section by section.

When this is done you may start the 4-2-4-2 rhythmic breathing.

When ready begin to build the Doorway into the Inner Worlds then walk over to the Door and open it.

Before you stands a tall figure robed in black and yellow, with a grave and sorrowful face. The eyes hold us so that we feel unable to move.

This is Uriel Archangel of the planet Earth. He has come to take us upon a journey that will have far-reaching effects upon us in the future.

The brilliant eyes draw the consciousness from us and we seem to fall through space for a long time before suddenly stopping.

Opening our eyes we find ourselves on a high plateau, the winds are so strong that they threaten to send us tumbling into the valley far below.

Uriel stands with us and points to the east. There we see coming towards us a billowing cloud made up of slender, ethereal creatures. In their midst is another and larger form.

They flutter around the archangel striving to get close to him as if his very presence is a joy to them.

The taller figure might have stepped from a fairy tale, tall and slender with a pointed elfin face with slanting silver eyes and pointed ears.

His hair is long and fair and moves constantly as if blown by an unfelt wind. He is wrapped in a cloak of misty blue.

He bows to Uriel and speaks, but we cannot understand him for his words are like great winds and soft breezes. Uriel touches our forehead with his finger and we find that suddenly we CAN understand what Paralda, the Elemental King of Air is saying, and we are able to speak in return.

He spreads his blue cloak over us and, with the sylphs following, he leaves the mountain, taking to the air.

The sudden movement outwards is frightening but this soon passes, and we know from his laughter that Paralda has enjoyed teasing us. Like all elemental creatures he can be mischieveous, but as the King of his element he alone is endowed with an immortal soul and this gives him the ability to love, laugh and understand.

We are carried over high mountains and down into deep valleys.

We sweep through forests and set the branches tossing like ships at sea.

We feel more at ease now for our human shape has changed and we are now like the sylphs. This makes us free of the need for Paralda's cloak.

We follow our companions swooping and diving as they do and for a while Paralda allows us this freedom.

We play like children, tossing newly-washed clothes about on their lines, ringing small bells in church belfries. We skim along the ground and lift fallen leaves high into the air, and pull scarves, umbrellas, and papers from clutching hands.

Then Paralda calls us to join him and we rest on a storm cloud that is heading out to sea.

Paralda tells us that not all his work is like this. Part of his domain is the weather, for movement of air is the basis of earth weather. The sylphs work closely with the element of water in order to keep the patterns flowing.

He tells us of the Trade Winds that blow in a precise pattern around the earth, and the way in which water-filled clouds are moved around to bring rain.

We learn that he is bound by the way in which the earth is tilted to bring more rain to some parts than others. He tells us that some people can influence weather patterns to a certain extent and delay rain or storm or, cause them to occur. While this is sometimes harmless it can also cause great damage.

He himself can be influenced by such people since he is subordinate to mankind in his power. He may understand that what is being demanded of him is wrong, but he cannot always disobey.

If rain is diverted from where it was supposed to be, then it must fall elsewhere, maybe on a ripening cornfield. The price of a sunny day for you can spell ruin for a farmer.

We ask about storms and hurricanes that cause damage and death.

Paralda explains that he is bound by the natural laws of cause and effect and by the force fields that surround earth. When a combination of events occurs he cannot evade the result. When the earth tilts away from the sun his element must cross areas that make the air cold. He cannot unmake winter, and a mixture of warm and cold together means fog that is natural law.

He tells us that the sylphs also exist within us, co-workers with us in life. Without them we could not breathe or speak or sing, yet we give little or no thanks for this. Only sometimes when we take a breath of clean sweet air we feel glad and they know then that we are aware of them.

But sylphs are changed by pollution and not happily. Through it they become other forms of existence that are neither beautiful nor useful, and which is against their primal pattern, degrading and crippling them.

Paralda rises and places his cloak about us and takes us back to Uriel to be made ready for the next part of our journey. He bids us farewell, bows to Uriel and with his followers returns to his work.

Uriel asks if we feel we have learned something from our talk with Paralda and we must answer as we feel . . .

Uriel folds us within the softness of his auric wings and there we cry on the heart of an archangel as we are taken back to our own place.

Uriel leaves us at the Door and before leaving blesses us, and with his hands on our head bids us REMEMBER.

We go through the Door and return to the physical body, awakening slowly and gently, looking around and noting the familiar things then gradually becoming fully aware once more.

Once you have made your recording (and are fully satisfied with the quality) you can proceed as you did with any other doorway. Find your quiet room and arrange that you will not be disturbed for the duration of the experiment. Sit in a comfortable chair and run through your conscious relaxation process.

This is, of course, an elemental pathworking and the fragment given is obviously associated with the element air. You might use the air *tattwa* (the blue circle) to enter this element; or, alternatively, you might seek to meet with Uriel in the Temple of Malkuth, where he has the right of access. In practice, however, neither of these approaches is particularly satisfactory.

The problem, of course, is that I have *extracted* only one section out of a far more balanced elemental working. Any attempt to use the air doorway will tend to unbalance it even further, while the Qabalistic temple – for reasons I do not entirely understand – is not entirely sympathetic to purely elemental experiences.

In her training video tape, Dolores Ashcroft-Nowicki creates a sort of general purpose astral doorway – a technique I had not come across before. This involves no more than the visualization of a stout doorway in the (physically blank) wall before you, opening it and, in your imagination, walking through.

When you are totally relaxed, switch on the tape, close your eyes and follow the instructions, allowing the images to arise. Since this is a guided working, and consequently somewhat safer than the more free-wheeling experience of the previous doorways, you might like to attempt a full projection using, for example, the Body of Light technique, before the taped journey begins. For this to be effective, you need to leave an introductory portion of the tape blank so that you have time to switch on, create and project into the Body of Light *before* the commentary begins.

Part Three
Projection In Practice

1.

Techniques of Projection

I began this workbook by remarking that the term *astral projection* is often loosely used to describe two experiences which are, in fact, separate and distinct: etheric projection and astral plane projection. Since you are unlikely to confuse the two again at this stage, the time has come to admit there are actually important links between them.

As you already know, various projectors have shown a tendency to slide from one form of projection into another. Robert Monroe, who certainly seemed to leave his body in the etheric, often found himself in a different (astral) world. And the Body of Light technique, an entirely astral operation, mimics an etheric projection so well that the two are often indistinguishable.

To use your astral (as distinct from etheric) body to explore the physical world requires you to break free of the astral environment. This is best achieved, as the Tibetan lamas continually stressed, by recognizing that the astral environment ultimately springs from the mind – if not your own mind, then some other. Even those stable astral areas which reflect physical plane formations are amenable to mental influence. On the Astral Plane, mind is *always* the overriding factor.

On this basis, moving from an astral environment back to the physical plane is really only a matter of will. But this is a little like saying that climbing Mount Everest is only a matter of will. The statement may be true, but it does not do most of us a lot of good.

In these circumstances, I can only advise you to work diligently towards a degree of insight, expertise and understanding that allows you to manipulate *any* astral environment at will, so that you may pass through the essential Astral *Light* to reach the physical plane any time you wish. But in the interim, you can always achieve the same results from a state of ignorance by a) tracking back from the Malkuth Temple or b) sinking down from the Sphere of Yesod. Although both these techniques are Qabalistic-based, you do not need to be a Qabalist to use them.

The Malkuth Temple is not something you establish – it exists permanently on the Astral Plane, thanks to the efforts of generations of Qabalists who built it there. Remember, out-of-body travel is largely a question of *thinking* yourself to a specific place, so the important factor is knowing where you are going.

Once you have a working knowledge of the Malkuth Temple, you can always return there quickly from *any* area of the Astral Plane. And since the Temple itself has intimate links with the physical plane (which it represents on the astral) returning to the physical plane from the Temple is very easy indeed. You can either create your own (imaginary) path between your body and the Temple, or, even more simply, allow the pillars of the Temple to dissolve into the walls of your room.

Even the small amount of information given in this book about the Tree of Life is enough to allow you to use it. The glyph claims to be a map of reality, and on a purely empirical basis you will quickly discover it is an accurate map so far as the relationship between the astral and physical planes are concerned. The (astral) Sphere of Yesod is shown as lying *above* the (physical) Sphere of Malkuth and this placement is correct . . . so long as you do not take it literally. Which brings me to something you will only really understand after you experience it. When you achieve a full, conscious, *etheric* projection, you will discover (once you start to look for it) that you have become aware of a new *direction.* Subjectively, this direction looks and feels like *upwards,* but it is not the same upwards you experience while in the physical body. (To confuse matters further, this physical upwards remains available to you, so that you can take out-of-body trips through the solar system and into Outer Space.)

The new upwards takes you directly – and recognizably – to the Astral Plane: it is the trip between Malkuth and Yesod, the Qabalistic thirty-second Path, the route taken by Dion Fortune in her dramatic experiment. Conversely, a peculiar sort of *downwards* sensed on the astral will allow you to float back to the physical world, where you can always reel in the silver cord in order to return to your body.

While I stand by my earlier statement that it is not *necessary* to study one form of projection in order to experience the other, the linkages between the two experiences make cross-fertilization *desirable.* For that reason, you may welcome the following integrated training programme, culled from the wealth of material previously given and designed to transform you into an experienced projector (etheric *and* astral plane) in the shortest possible time.

Astral Projection Workbook Integrated Training Programme

Step 1: Conscious Relaxation

Before attempting *anything* else, work to achieve conscious relaxation. This is the absolute foundation of so much work on projection that it is difficult to imagine your making any real progress without it. Relaxation is discussed in depth in the section of the workbook concerned with etheric projection. Read it now if you have not already done so. As a convenient reference, the useful technique given in that section, which includes breath control, is repeated below.

Begin by regulating your breathing. Relaxation is a physical function. Your muscles use oxygen extracted from your bloodstream. Your bloodstream, in turn, extracts that oxygen from the air you breathe. By regulating your breathing, you increase the oxygen available in your blood, your muscles extract the optimum amount and are far happier to relax for you than they might otherwise be.

If you have studied yoga, you will know there are all sorts of complex breath-regulation techniques. But the one I want you to try is very simple. It is called 2/4 breathing.

What it comes down to is that you

1. Breathe in to the mental count of four . . .
2. Hold your breath in to the mental count of two . . .
3. Breathe out to the mental count of four . . .
4. Hold your breath out to the mental count of two.

The rate at which you should count varies from individual to individual. Start by synchronizing it with your heartbeat. If this doesn't work, play around until you hit on the rhythm that is most comfortable for you.

Get your breathing comfortable before you go on to the second part of the exercise.

Once you have established a comfortable rhythm of 2/4 breathing, let it run for about three minutes, then start the following relaxation sequence. (If you can hold the 2/4 rhythm while you do it, that's great, but chances are you will not be able to do so at first. In this latter case, just start your session with three minutes of 2/4 breathing, then go back to normal breathing while you carry out the main relaxation sequence, then take up 2/4 breathing again when you are nicely relaxed.)

Concentrate on your feet. Wiggle them about; curl them to tense the muscles, then allow them to relax.

Concentrate next on your calf muscles. Tighten and relax them.

Concentrate on your thigh muscles. Tighten and relax them.

Concentrate on your buttock muscles. Tighten your buttocks and anus, then relax them.

Concentrate on your stomach muscles, a very common tension focus. Tighten then relax them.

Concentrate on your hands. Curl them into fists, then relax them.

Concentrate on your arms. Tighten them rigidly, then relax them.

Concentrate on your back. Tighten the muscles, then relax them.

Concentrate on your chest. Tighten the muscles, then relax them.

Concentrate on your shoulders, another very common tension focus. Hunch your shoulders to tighten the muscles, then relax them.

Concentrate on your neck. Tighten the muscles then relax them.

Concentrate on your face. Grit your teeth and contort your features to tense up the facial muscles then relax them.

Concentrate on your scalp. Frown to tighten the scalp muscles, then relax them.

Now tighten up every muscle in your body, holding your entire body momentarily rigid, then relax, letting go as completely as you are able. Do this final whole body sequence again, then again – three times in all. On the third time, take a really deep breath when you tense the muscles and sigh deeply aloud as you let the tension go.

You should be feeling nicely relaxed by now. If you abandoned your 2/4 breathing at the start of the relaxation sequence, pick it up again at this point.

Close your eyes and try to imagine your whole body getting heavier and heavier, as if it were turning to lead. You will find your visualization increases your level of relaxation still further.

Enjoy the sensation of relaxation for the remainder of your session. But stay vigilant. Should you find tension creeping in anywhere (and you certainly will in the early days) don't let it worry you. Just tighten up the tense muscles a little more, then relax them.

Use the technique regularly until you have trained yourself to relax totally any time you want to.

Following the advice in that final sentence may take quite a lot of time, but do please persevere. Spend *at least* two weeks on daily relaxation practice before you move on to the next stage; and continue to set aside a period each day to practise relaxation thereafter. You can speed your progress by adding small 'catch-exercises' outside your formal relaxation period. If at any time during the day you notice yourself tense, take time to let go for a moment so that relaxation eventually becomes a reflex.

Step 2: Visualization

Practise visualization. I have never had the slightest trouble creating mental pictures and I tend to underestimate the problems they can cause others. On one occasion I actually met a graphic artist who could not visualize. I would have thought this impossible, yet she assured me it was so. She could draw and paint representationally, and do so extremely well, but pictures in the mind were beyond her. Fortunately this ability, like so many other things, is as much practice as talent.

If you find your natural degree of visualization fuzzy, then simply add 10 minutes visualization practice to your regular relaxation sessions. Pick your scene or object and work at 'seeing' it more clearly. It is a good idea to test yourself by forcing your attention onto details. Count the number of buttons on a coat, for example, or the number of blades of grass in a tuft.

If your natural degree of visualization is non-existant – like that of my friend the graphic artist – a good place to start is by staring at a simple picture long enough to develop an after-image when you look away. (Experiment until you find one that suits you.) Then close your eyes and examine the after-image on your darkened visual field. This image is very similar to visualization and can usually be interiorized without too much difficulty. Variations on the technique are, of course, used in several of the astral doorways mentioned earlier.

Whatever your natural degree of ability to begin with, you will certainly find it improves with practice. But do not stop with developing your *visual* imagination. Imagine how an object feels to the touch. See if you can mentally pick up scents. Listen to imaginary sounds. Ideally, you should train your inner vision to a pitch where you can easily imagine *anything*. Sometimes this leads to odd situations. Physically, I have almost no sense of smell – the olfactory equivalent of colour blindness. But I still have no difficulty imagining smells – even those I can no longer pick up physically.

It is difficult to say how long you are going to need to bring your powers of visualization to a working peak but, as with relaxation, *regular* practice is important. As a minimum, devote two weeks to improving natural visualization or as long as it takes to develop visualization if none comes naturally to you. But you can, as I mentioned earlier, combine these preliminary exercises with your relaxation practice.

Step 3: Loosening the Subtle Bodies

Sylvan Muldoon's chronic illness seems to have blessed (or perhaps cursed) him with a naturally loose etheric body. I suspect, from the ease with which I took to inner plane operations, the same might be said about my own astral vehicle. Whatever the natural state of your subtle bodies, they can be loosened *before* you embark on any projection experiments. The method of doing so forms part of a broader esoteric technique known as the Christos Experience. You will need three people to carry it through – the subject, who may be you, and two helpers. The relevant steps are as follows:

1. Begin by having your subject lie flat on his back on the floor. Put a small cushion or pillow under his head so his neck is straight and he can lie comfortably. Have him remove his shoes. Socks, stockings or tights may be left on. In this position, the subject closes his eyes.

2. Have your helper begin gently to massage the subject's ankles. A light, circular motion on the ankle bones is what is required here. Until you actually experience it, you will find it difficult to imagine how extraordinarily relaxing this is.

3. After about a minute, and while the ankle massage is still going on, place the edge of your curved hand on the subject's forehead so that it rests between the eyes, fitting snugly into the hollow at the root of the nose. In this position, it covers the traditional site of the Third Eye. This location is the spot highlighted by the Hindu caste mark.

Once your hand is in position and with the ankle massage continuing, begin a vigorous circular rubbing movement which should be continued until your subject reports that his head is buzzing. Make sure he remains fully relaxed. If tension has crept in, have him take several deep breaths and go limp.

This concludes the physical aspect of the method, although ankle massage continued very gently throughout the remainder of the session helps the subject to stay relaxed.

4. The mental aspect of the method now begins. Instruct your subject to keep his eyes shut and *visualize his feet*. He should try to make this (and all subsequent visualizations) as vivid as possible, so long as the effort to do so does not spoil his relaxation.

5. Have him tell you when he has managed to visualize his feet successfully,

then instruct him to imagine himself growing two inches (about five centimetres) longer through the soles of his feet. He should try to feel the sensation of growing and see the result in his mind's eye.

6. Wait until the subject tells you he has managed to achieve Stage 5, then instruct him to return to his usual length. He should try to imagine the sight and feel of his feet returning towards him in their normal position.

7. Repeat this process at least three times – and more if necessary – until your subject is fully accustomed to it and can visualize the peculiar 'growth' with practised ease. Don't hurry this: it is a very important part of the overall process and one that lays the foundation of much that is to follow. Wait each time until your subject tells you he has been successful. Your patience at this point will be amply rewarded later.

8. Now repeat the whole process, but this time your subject is required to grow through the *top of his head* then return to his normal size. If you have taken the time to run him properly through the foot process, this should be fairly easy. Once again, repeat it at least three times.

9. Return your subject's attention to his feet and ask him to 'grow' out *12* inches (30 centimetres) this time and return to his normal length. Make certain he has done this successfully before moving on.

10. Repeat the 12 inch growth and shrinkage through the top of the head.

11. Return your attention to the feet and now ask your subject to grow out *24* inches (60 centimetres). Interestingly, the fact that someone can successfully make a mental two inch stretch does not automatically guarantee he will be able to go further. Have him keep trying until he manages the 24 inch stretch (which should be accomplished in under a minute) *but do not have him return to normal size.*

12. While your subject feels he has stretched 24 inches through the soles of his feet, have him *simultaneously* stretch 24 inches through the top of his head. Weird though it may sound, some subjects find that as they start to stretch through their heads at this point, their extended feet begin to withdraw. Persevere until the two-way stretch is achieved and here again *do not* have your subject return to normal size.

13. While at full stretch through head and feet, ask your subject to expand all over, as if he was blowing up like a balloon. Keep trying until he can feel himself extended beyond the limits of his physical body. We tend to think of swelling as associated with malaise or discomfort, but in this instance the sensation is very pleasant once the extension has been achieved.

14. With Stage 13, the loosening process is complete. The subject may proceed directly to an attempt at etheric or astral plane projection. If projection is *not* to be attempted right away, *make absolutely sure to instruct the subject to imagine himself returning to his normal size.* Failure to do so can lead to problems.

Step 4: Dream Awareness

Although there are many other options open, you can use the mind-awake/body-asleep state as the key to both etheric and astral plane projections. The most direct route to this state is dream control. And the first stage of dream control is heightened awareness of your dreams. Buy yourself that notebook or tape recorder suggested in the text and develop the habit of recording your night's dreams immediately on waking.

Dream analysis is a useful and important art on its own, but one which lies well beyond the scope of this book. For the purpose of projection, your only interest is to increase your conscious awareness of your world of dreams and to take note of any flying dreams that may arise. Continue the process until a habit is well established, probably over the course of a month.

Step 5: Dream Control

Now the time has come to seize control of your night-life. The time to do so is when you enter that pleasant, drifting, hypnogogic state between waking and sleep. The way to do so is self-suggestion.

At this point, of course, you will have to decide whether you wish first to develop etheric projection, astral plane projection or, possibly, both more or less simultaneously. But whatever your choice, I would recommend that your initial effort in dream control is aimed towards becoming *conscious* that you are dreaming. This step takes you directly into a subjective astral plane environment, but is also makes it a great deal easier for you to construct the sort of flying dreams Muldoon has recommended as an etheric projection trigger.

Once you become self-aware in a dream, you have the choice of going on to develop your astral plane skills, or, having constructed your flying dream, awakening yourself in the physical world . . . hopefully in your projected etheric body.

Since dream control is the key to so much, you can afford to make a heavy investment of time and energy into its development. It is not easy and some people never manage it, but I would recommend three to six months of effort before you even consider abandoning the attempt. This is a worst-case scenario, of course; you may get lucky and develop dream control in a week.

If, after giving it your best shot, you still find dream control beyond you, move on to the other techniques given in this workbook.

Step 6: Body of Light

However well you do with dream control, I would suggest you take the trouble to perfect the Body of Light technique. It is your link between etheric and astral plane projections, since the Body of Light may be used for either.

Two to three weeks preliminary visualization practice will prepare you for the experiment, a further one to two weeks should be enough to establish the Body of Light, and a final week or so of daily practice should give you the knack of transferring consciousness to it.

2.

The Ultimate Projection

What good is all this? Is out-of-body experience just an appealing self-indulgence, or can it be developed into something so important that the Government will some day feel compelled to tax it?

A variety of possibilities arise out of the techniques given in this book. The chapter on the *I Ching*, for example, gives all the information necessary for practising the ancient art of magical evocation. Combine those techniques with an extension of the *tulpa* creation essential to the Body of Light and you could even end up with evocation *to visible appearance* – a highly advanced magical operation.

Perhaps your interests lie in alchemy, that most obscure of occult arts. If so, you might like to find out what would happen if the physical aspects of alchemical experiments were combined with the astral operations given in the old textbooks.

If these pathways seem a little weird, you might find more of interest in the possibility that an out-of-body physician could do more to heal certain conditions than his counterpart burdened by all-too-solid flesh. Or, more immediately, you could follow the example of one projector mentioned earlier in this book, who slips out of her body when she is required to undergo painful medical treatment. She remains close enough to monitor what is going on and can influence her body to answer any necessary questions, but the pain itself is removed from her.

Manipulation of the Astral Plane (whether or not you are actually projected) can produce a host of benefits, as every practising magician knows. These vary from spiritual development to making money.

For some reason a great many occultists are too embarrassed to talk about the latter techniques, so you will have to search for them among those frenzied books which seem to promise instant riches while you cat-nap. Their authors seldom realize they are engaged in astral operations, but they are.

If you prefer to make your living by the sweat of your brow, you could do worse than study the life of Nikola Tesla, the prolific Yugoslav-American inventor of, among other things, alternating current. Tesla has such a natural grasp of astral manipulation that he could build an entire machine in the vivid world of his imagination, set it running in his mind, go about his business for three weeks, then break down the astral machine and inspect its component parts for wear. This enabled him to predict precisely how such a machine would behave if it were built physically.

I could go on and on, but there is one area in which experience gained out of the body will prove absolutely invaluable to you. Please forgive me for mentioning it, but even you will die one day. When you do, this is what will happen:

First, barring accident or murder, you will die slowly. The process starts at the cellular level and goes on to embrace the organs. For the first 20 years of your life, your cells are engaged in growth. Thereafter they begin a very gentle backslide. Those you lose in wear and tear of daily living are replaced less and less efficiently. Eventually they are not replaced at all. The end result takes a long time – anything up to a maximum of a hundred years or so – but is absolutely predictable just the same. Our culture likes to call the process *aging*. The reality is that you are engaged in dying.

For much of the time, the process is not particularly noticeable, even if you look very, very closely. An optical microscope shows nothing until your problems become gross. With an electron microscope, however, it is easier to see what is going on. The fine structures of the cell become noticeably disrupted. Swelling often appears, followed by rupture of cell contents into the surrounding tissue. Alternatively, the cell nucleus alone may swell and rupture, fragment, or even shrink. Either way, the bottom line is cell death. You will, of course, be unaware of what is happening to your individual cells. But the mirror will tell you that you are growing old.

Insurance companies do not accept old age as a cause of death. They look for even more immediate factors like heart failure, as if to insist that death is actually an illness rather than a natural process. But while terminal illness is often a feature of death, it is not a necessary prerequisite. Nor is discomfort or terror. It is a curious fact that the closer you get to death from extreme old age, the less fear you have of it.

Of course, many old people suffer from senility and sink into semi-conscious conditions where fear of death is avoided by living in the past. But where extreme old age is accompanied by lucidity, a calm acceptance seems to be the psychological norm. By then you will already have lost many, perhaps most, of your friends and relatives, so the final loss of life itself may not seem too bad.

Whatever the reason, there are clear indications that in this stage you retain a certain amount of control. You will be able, within reason, to select the moment of your death. You can postpone it for a few hours or days in order to complete unfinished business. Or you can embrace it willingly when you decide your time has come.

Your time will not come, however, all at once. Just as you are destined to die slowly, so you are also destined to die piecemeal. The human organism does not break down all at once. You might, for example, survive for hours, perhaps even days, after the demise of your liver or kidneys. Even the cessation of your heart – that old medical determinant of death – is not definitive: your brain will continue to function for a further four minutes before damage caused by lack of oxygen becomes irreversible.

Because of this, you will be trouble to the very last. At a time when your heart has stopped, your eyes dimmed, your breathing halted and the woes of the world ceased to concern you, those by your bedside may still have difficulty determining whether you have actually left them. Their problem is that several conditions – coma is one well-known example – closely mimic death. Too many breathless, pulseless people have subsequently awakened for the doctors to get cocky.

But if your harassed physicians are prepared to wait, the problem will become self-solving. There are certain signs which *only* occur in the presence of death. Thus, your final medical examination will begin with a search for a peripheral pulse at wrist or throat. Failing to find any, the doctors will check for a heartbeat. Finding this too is absent, they may now note that your breathing has stopped and your mouth, lips and extremities are turning blue.

If you happen to be wired up to an electroencephalograph, the trace which previously featured a lively series of peaks and valleys will flatten out within the next five minutes, indicating brain death. The doctors will test for certain eye reflexes . . . which will be found missing.

Even now, though no one would bet on it, there is a slim chance your condition may not be terminal. But then will come the signs which brook no argument, the indelible imprint of the Reaper's hand.

The first is *algor mortis:* your body temperature falls to that of your immediate environment. Next comes *rigor mortis,* a temporary rigidity of the skeletal muscles. Then *livor mortis* rears its ugly head as parts of your body exhibit the purple-red discolouration of blood settling. . . And if anyone retains the slightest doubt, that too will soon be laid to rest as indications of microbial attack become evident. There is no delicate way to put it. You will begin to rot. At this point, you may be certain you are completely, utterly, irreversibly dead. You may not have found the process pleasant, but at least what happens next is interesting.

I have information to suggest that if you die of old age in full health, the fundamental sensation is one of unmitigated relief – a relaxation and a letting go. If you are terminally ill, however, the immediate lead-up to death tends to be a progression of physical discomfort. This is not necessarily – indeed not usually – pain. The body has several mechanisms which supress terminal pain very effectively. But discomfort remains and peaks at the point of death.

Your exact experience of the moment depends on a variety of factors, among them your level of body awareness, the type of illness (if any) you suffered, and whether or not you have been given consciousness-dimming drugs.

Many medical preparations and certain types of illness (notably those of a feverish or comatose nature) block your awareness of the process of transition, as, of course, does dying in your sleep. Or you may be the type of person whose body awareness is low, who simply does not notice the finer detail of what is happening to you. But assuming your perceptions are keen, awake and undistracted, you will notice a peculiar buzzing or ringing sound, sometimes followed by a metallic clang. For a brief, disorienting moment, you will feel you are rushing through a darkened tunnel.

The tunnel is real enough, although it is not actually a tunnel at all. At death, your centre of consciousness moves from its usual seat behind your eyes, upwards and backwards to vacate the body via one of two predictable locations on the skull. This movement is swift. When it happens, it creates the illusion of rushing through a tunnel.

But everything is happening with such speed you may not notice the tunnel effect at all. At much the same time this is going on, your collection of subtle bodies – etheric, astral, mental, spiritual – are separating as a unit from the physical. Your consciousness homes in on them like a racing pigeon.

For those ignorant of things like subtle bodies, this can be a time of considerable confusion for as you now know, you do not feel very different in the etheric than you do in the physical. For this reason, many people do not – at least at first – realize they are dead. In fact, they generally feel very well, since the symptoms of illness do not carry over. In this state they try vainly to attract the attention of mourners and generally give themselves a very hard time until the truth dawns.

In your case, however, things will be a lot easier. As an etheric projector, the experience of death will be very familiar to you – the only immediate difference being that the silver cord no longer attaches you to the physical body. But that is an important difference, for without the physical linkage, your etheric body will eventually begin to disintegrate as well, releasing the astral vehicle onto its own plane of operation, the Astral Plane.

Here again, your skill as a projector will be of considerable benefit to you. As you are now aware, the Astral Plane reflects your unconscious expectations – and at no time so powerfully as when you visit after death. For this reason, your cultural conditioning (and poor self-image) might well have landed you in one of the astral hells. But it would have been a hell of your own making, just as the many astral heavens are no more than external reflections of the individual's own psychic state.

As a projector with experience of the Astral Plane, you can avoid both traps and . . . what? The answer to that tricky little question really does depend on quite how far you pushed your experience of the Inner Planes while you were still in incarnation. You may have used your astral trips to investigate the possibility of reincarnation. Or you may have followed Dion Fortune up the planes to realms of Cosmic Light.

Whatever information you gathered as an astral projector, I suspect it will be of considerable importance to you in the post-mortem state. And that's something you can't say of very many other occupations.

Appendix

Questions and Answers

The idea of projection – however defined – worries people. Leaving your body, for whatever destination, is too closely associated with death for comfort. But what, if anything, can go wrong? Over the years, I have fielded quite a few questions posed by nervous projectors, actual and prospective. Some of the more common – and their answers – are appended below.

What happens if I can't get back into my body?
Failure to get back into your physical body would obviously be big trouble . . . if it happened. Fortunately, most projectors find the real problem is staying out, not getting back in. In years of work in the field, I have yet to find a single projector – astral plane or etheric – who reported the slightest difficulty in getting back into the physical body.

Interestingly, I have worked with one or two projectors who were in considerable physical pain due to injury or illness. Since they were usually unaware of their pain in the projected state, they had considerable motivation to stay out of the physical for as long as possible. Even in these conditions, re-entry into the physical proved all to easy.

Is it possible to lose awareness of the physical body?
Yes, easily. With both forms of projection, awareness of the physical body is usually lost quite quickly. This is nothing to worry about. Indeed, successful projections seems to *require* loss of awareness of the physical body.

What happens if I can't *find my way back* to my physical body?
This is an altogether more important question and one which requires two different answers, depending on whether you are engaged in etheric or astral plane projection.

In etheric projection, close proximity to the physical body sets up a pull which tends to snap the (projected) etheric body back into the physical. Once you move six to ten feet away from the physical body, however, this pull lessens to the point where it is unnoticeable. And since it is extremely easy to travel while projected, there are a few problems in finding yourself a considerable geographical distance from where your physical body is lying. At such times, it is possible to become confused about the direction you need to travel in order to return to the physical.

But confusion, however extreme, will not change two fundamental facts. The first is that however far you move away, you still remain attached to the physical body by the 'silver cord' mentioned frequently in the text of the workbook. The second is that while in the projected state, it is enough to think of a destination in order to go there – in other words, thought and travel are closely interlinked.

Given these two facts, finding your way back to your physical body during an etheric projection is fairly straightforward. If you are aware of the silver cord, you can use it to haul yourself in, so to speak, like a fish. If you are not aware of the cord (and some projectors aren't) then your simplest approach is to think about returning to your body and you will find you automatically do so. For the fastest possible return, you can adopt Robert Monroe's suggestion that you attempt to move some part of your physical body, such as a finger or toe. This has the effect of drawing the etheric back into the physical very quickly.

If the problem of finding your way back troubles you a lot, then it is a good idea to practise these return techniques while you are still comparatively close to your physical body and know perfectly well how to return to it anyway. Once you get the hang of returning by willing it, or signalling your physical body to move from a distance, you can project further out with greater confidence. And just as I have never personally found anyone who had trouble getting back into their body, so I have never found anyone who had any real difficulty finding their body during an etheric projection.

Some experts believe the same holds true of astral plane projection. One occultist of my acquaintance with considerable astral plane experience is on record with the statement that it is quite impossible to become lost on the Astral Plane since the (physical) body pull is too strong to allow it to happen.

I suspect this may be true eventually – if you remain on the Astral Plane long enough for your physical body to become hungry, for example, there will be a growing call for you to return. Short term, however, my experience has been that it is perfectly possible to get lost on the Astral Plane; and the experience is often frightening.

Prevention is always a lot easier than cure; and prevention in this context is very simple. Take careful note of your astral surroundings and do not move into new areas until you are familiar with your immediate environment. Since astral plane projection often involves the use of a doorway, make certain it is firmly established in the Astral Plane before you move away and watch out for landmarks.

Should you plan an extensive astral plane journey, you can solve the orienteering problems completely by *leaving a trail*. Since astral matter is so easily manipulated by thought and visualization, you can spin a thread behind you like a spider, or simply leave a trail of glowing arrows pointing the way back to your doorway.

Another useful approach (and one which I adopted in my early astral plane experiments) is to make certain you do not project unless there is someone present to look after your physical body. Your companion can talk you back home if you are away too long or if you show signs of discomfort.

Finally, to reinforce the earlier point, if all else fails, make yourself comfortable on the astral and wait. Sooner or later the call of hunger or even more urgent body functions will draw you back in. It may be a nerve-wracking adventure, but at least it will have a happy ending.

Is it possible to meet dangerous or threating entities while in the projected state?

The truthful answer seems to be yes, with reservations.

First, I may as well say that this has never happened to any subject I have worked with during an *etheric* projection. Etheric projectors, in my experience, are always aware of people (animals and places) on the physical and *sometimes* aware of people who are, like themselves, operating out of their physical bodies. I have no reports of alien (i.e. non-human) entities in this state, nor of any threat or danger posed by the disembodied people who did occasionally make an appearance.

Having said this, a reading of the literature on the subject will soon indicate not everyone has shared this placid experience of etheric projection. Monroe, for example, writes of a variety of threatening experiences while projected. To say there may be some confusion between etheric and astral plane projection in reports of this type is really of little help to anyone caught up in a frightening situation. But Monroe himself has made the important point that after decades of regular projections, he is still here to tell the tale – which suggests that out of body threats may be more frightening than dangerous.

Astral plane projection can, in my experience, lead much more frequently to the appearance of non-human entities and some of these encounters are likely to appear threatening, or even dangerous. How dangerous they may actually be, I do not really know – except to say I have never lost an astral plane projector yet. But they can certainly be frightening.

Perhaps the easiest way of coping with them is to keep calm, remember where you are and remember the peculiar laws of the Astral Plane. One projector I worked with was approached on the Astral Plane by a very threatening entity with all the unpleasant characteristics of a fairy tale ogre, including a hefty club. I have no idea what might have transpired had she panicked, but in the event she kept calm, waited until he was quite close, then leaped over his head and went her way. Since you can do comic-book stuff like this on the Astral Plane, and even shape-shift if you need to, it seems quite unlikely that you will meet anything which can do you real harm if you keep your head.

Two further points need to be made. The first is that in an extreme situation, you always have the option of fleeing to your physical body – a return trip that can be made instantaneously. The second is a reminder that your astral environment mirrors your own interests. In *Astral Doorways* I made this much-quoted point that if you met anything nasty on the Astral Plane, it was because there was something nasty in your head to begin with. This is perhaps a little simplistic, but important nonetheless. Anyone with a knowledge of a major city knows perfectly well that if you go walking alone at night in certain districts, you are asking for trouble. The same holds true for the Astral Plane, except that the districts can be creations of your own mind.

Can projections over a long period make me ill?

The bottom line answer seems to be no, so long as you are talking about *physical* illness. But even here the situation is a little complicated.

As you have already noted, physical illness or accident can actually be an aid to projection. Sylvan Muldoon suffered chronic illness over many years and clearly believed his infirmity helped him slip out of his body at will. Accidents, such as a car crash, can sometimes catapult the etheric body out of the physical. Acute illnesses can also force a projection, as Jung's heart attack did when he found himself in orbit around the planet. Near-death experiences are almost invariably accompanied by projection, astral plane or etheric (and sometimes both.)

From all this, it is clear that there is a solid connection between illness or injury and out-of-body experience. But the connection does seem to be one-way. That is to say, physical illness or accident may lead to projection, but projection does not appear to lead to physical illness.

There is some indication that repeated projections may 'loosen' the subtle bodies. Certainly the more often you project, the easier it becomes. But there is no evidence that the loosening effect (if it really occurs) is actually harmful to your health.

None of this is to say that there are *no* health problems associated with projection. Too abrupt a return to your physical body can cause headache, jarring sensations, muscle spasm and, in rare cases, bone fracture. (The latter is similar to cough fractures and just as unusual.) It is also true to say that if you have a pre-existent condition – such as a weak heart – the stresses of projection may prove harmful, as may stress of any sort. But these are peripheral reactions and every indication is that if you treat projection sensibly, avoiding the more obvious risk areas, then it is as safe as most occupations and safer than many where your physical well-being is concerned.

A word of warning may, however, be appropriate in relation to your *psychological* health. Astral plane projection is sometimes seized upon by certain types of personality as an escape from the 'real' (i.e. physical) world. Typically, such personalities tend to be misfits in their society, or at least unsuccessful in terms of their career, and/or human relationships, but the excitement and glamour of astral experience presents a risk for almost anyone. The literature of occultism is replete with warnings about the dangers of astral glamour, a clear indication that multitudes of occultists have fallen prey to it.

Those who succumb to the fascination become, to a greater or lesser extent, astral junkies, soaking themselves in the glittering fantasies of the plane as often as possible. Since the resurgence of interest in occultism which accompanied the hippy movement of the Sixties, the astral junkie has often been a drug junkie as well, using psychedelics to gain entry into the plane.

Avoidance of psychological damage is largely a matter of common sense prevention. No one who refuses absolutely to sample drugs (even once) ever becomes addicted to them. And since drugs are absolutely unnecessary for astral plane (or, indeed, etheric) projection there can be no excuse whatsoever for their use.

Freedom from fascination is, admittedly, a little more difficult, for the Astral Plane is a fascinating place. (It has certainly drawn me back time and time again over the years.) But acceptance of its fascination is one thing: being overwhelmed by that fascination is quite another. The trick is to keep a sense of proportion. Your investigations of the astral are no more important than the work you do to earn a living. The plane itself is a dimension with no more to teach than the physical dimension in which we live. Astral travellers are not supermen or superwomen. At most they are research students in a neglected field.

Is projection sinful?

Apparently not.

Although few churches admit to an offical policy on the subject, esoteric practice is generally frowned upon by the religious establishment, on the grounds that it can lead to interest or dabbling in the 'black' arts, or become a substitute for the individual's religion. Clearly, this blanket disapproval must extend to the techniques of projection, yet projection *per se* is too closely interwoven with religious experience to be branded sinful.

This is particularly evident in the projections associated with near-death experience. As we have seen in the body of the workbook, such projections often have religious overtones: reports of meetings with luminous, Christ-like figures are almost commonplace. But even leaving aside such overt experiences, there is little argument that successful projection strongly reinforces the (religious) doctrine of post mortem survival. For this reason, I suspect, the phenomenon has attracted the attention of many clerics.

Another factor arises from a study of the lives of saints. One pointer towards sainthood is a talent for something called *bilocation*. Bilocation, as the word itself suggests, is defined as the ability to be in two different places at the same time. A number of historical saints have exhibited this curious talent. Typically, such saints have been monastics and their abilities tend to come to light when they are seen in distant places (such as the bedside of a dying Pope) while meditating in the solitude of their cells.

Often enough, the saints themselves have been unable to explain this curious phenomenon, but to anyone who has studied projection, the mechanics are quite clear. An individual in solitary, silent meditation is well placed to project. If, at the time of projection, the individual's thoughts are fixed on some distant event – such as a battle or the death of a religious superior – the movement of the second body to the site of that event is automatic. The first (physical) body remains in meditation posture in the cell. The second (astral or etheric) flies to the distant destination.

Against this background, it seems safe to suggest that while no amount of projection will make you a saint, no one can reasonably claim it will make you a sinner either.

Can I be seen when I am in a projected state?
Generally no, but there are exceptions.

This question relates almost exclusively to etheric projection, since astral plane projection does not normally bring you into contact with anyone outside of the plane itself.

During an etheric projection, you will be invisible and intangible to almost all of those who remain within the physical body. This is a factor which can cause considerable distress during the ultimate etheric projection at the point of death. Spiritualist communication is full of descriptions of individuals who, having died without realizing, try desperately to reassure sorrowing relatives at the bedside, only to find their best efforts are ignored.

But if most people are unable to see you, a surprising number are able to sense your presence to some degree. This manifests (for the individual visited) as a feeling of unease, of 'being watched' or threatened, or, less often, as a perception of chill. The same sensations, perhaps not too surprisingly, are often associated with visitations by ghosts.

Certain talented individuals – commonly referred to as psychics – will be aware of your presence at once and there is considerable evidence to suggest that should you visit someone with whom you are emotionally intimate, such as a blood relative, spouse or lover, the chances of your being seen increase. It seems too that your *intent* will influence the situation. If it is your desire to communicate and be seen, the likelihood of being seen increases.

Most animals are far more sensitive to projective visitations than human beings. Cats, in particular, seem to be able to see projected bodies without much difficulty, although they are as likely to ignore you in your projected state as they are while you occupy a physical body. Dogs too will often sense a projection and are, in general, more disturbed by the experience than cats.

Can I go anywhere I want while projected?
Not entirely. Projection certainly opens up far wider (and cheaper!) travel opportunities than you enjoy in the physical body. As you have seen in the workbook, Arthur Gibson was quite capable of travelling from Ireland to India almost instantaneously and a surprisingly large number of projectors claim to have left not only the planet, but the actual solar system and journeyed to worlds in distant galaxies. Such trips suggest that projection not only over-comes the need for support systems like air, heat and atmospheric pressure, but may actually allow you to travel faster than the speed of light – a theoretical absolute in the physical universe.

Despite all this, experience will eventually indicate there are certain places you simply cannot go. Elsewhere, I mentioned the experience of my wife who visited the home of friends while in a projected state and tried to enter their bedroom to give them the exciting news. She found herself unable to do so and later discovered they were engaged in sexual intercourse at the time she called, hence the need of privacy. The interesting thing here is that the need seems to have set up some sort of invisible barrier through which my wife, in her projected state, was quite unable to pass.

Such barriers may be more commonplace than we imagine. Projection has been a fact of human life throughout history and presumably before, but I have yet to find a single instance of information gathered during projection being used, for example, as an aid to blackmail. It may be that when we embark on those activities of which we are ashamed, or which we simply wish to remain private, we throw up instinctive safeguards against subtle visitations. Although this is, perhaps, a natural mechnism, there are suggestions from a strange quarter that it may have been tamed and put to use as an artifact. These suggestions are embodied in the techniques of ritual magic.

This workbook is eccentric enough without wishing to delve too deeply into the realms of ritual. Suffice to say that almost every ritual magical operation begins with a 'preparation of the place', analogous to the sterilization of the theatre before a surgical operation begins.

Typical of the means used to prepare for a major ceremonial is the subsidiary ritual of the banishing pentagram. For those of you interested in such things, the pentagram ritual is carried out as follows:

Preparation
Room
Clear a room. If you can't do this fully, push the furniture aside so you have a large clear space in the centre. Begin by learning the sub-ritual of the Qabalistic Cross.

Qabalistic Cross sub-ritual:

Outer Working
1. Raise your right hand to a point about three inches *above* your head.
2. Bring your hand down to touch your forehead.
3. As you touch your forehead vibrate the word *Ah-Teh*.
4. Bring the hand down to touch your breastbone.
5. Vibrate *Mal-Kuth*.
6. Touch your right shoulder.
7. Vibrate *Veh-Geb-Your-Ah*.
8. Bring the hand across to touch your left shoulder.
9. Vibrate *Veh-Ged-You-Lah*.
10. Clasp your hands together in the form of a cup at a level with your chest.
11. Vibrate *Lay-Oh-Eem*.
12. Vibrate *Ah-Men*.

Inner Working
Standing upright, arms by sides, relaxed as possible, visualize a glowing sphere of luminous white light (about the size of a child's football) floating a few inches above the crown of your head.

At 1. touch this sphere with your upraised hand.

As you draw your hand downwards to touch your forehead, visualize a shaft of brilliant white light emerging from the sphere to pierce your body.

As you touch your chest as 4. the shaft of light should be visualized as extending all the way through your body to end between your feet, so that you are now totally transfixed by a pillar of glowing white light.

At 6. visualize a second, somewhat smaller sphere on a level with your right shoulder, partly interpenetrating the shoulder. Think of this sphere as a reservoir of energy.

As you bring your hand across at 8. visualize yourself drawing a second shaft of brilliant white light from the right shoulder (Geburah) sphere across and through your body to link up with a similar sphere at your left shoulder.

At this point, if you have visualized correctly, you will be transfixed by a massive cross of brilliant light.

At 10. visualize a small, steady blue flame between your cupped hands.

This completes the Ritual of the Qabalistic Cross. A magical pentagram is drawn in the following manner:

Hand:

Make a fist. Point with your forefinger. Now point simultaneously with the next finger. Your hand is now as it should be for drawing and stabbing the pentagram.

Start here

Draw the pentagram as shown, using the outstretched fingers of your right hand. Start at about the level of your left hip. Carry the upward sweep above your head, come down to your right hip level and continue until the figure is complete. Don't draw it in any other sequence.

The full banishing ritual of the pentagram is as follows:

Outer Working
1. Walk to the eastern quarter of the room and face east.
2. Perform the entire Qabalistic Cross ritual, inner and outer workings.
3. Trace a pentagram in the air before you.
4. Stab the pentagram through the centre with your outstretched fingers.
5. As you do so, vibrate *Yod-Heh-Vav-Heh*.
6. With your arm outstretched, move clockwise to the south.
7. Trace a second pentagram, stab it and vibrate *Ah-Doh-Nay*.

8. With arm outstetched, move clockwise to the west.

9. Trace a third pentagram, stab it and vibrate *Eh-Heh-Yeh*.

10. With arm outstetched, move clockwise to the north.

11. Trace a fourth pentagram, stab it and vibrate *Aye-Geh-Lah*.

12. Return to the east and complete the circle by bringing your outstetched fingers to the centre of the first pentagram.

13. Stretch your arms out sideways to you stand in the form of a cross.

14. Vibrate *Before me Rah-Fi-El*.

15. Vibrate *Behind me Gah-Brah-El*.

16. Vibrate *At my right hand Me-Kah-El*.

17. Vibrate *At my left hand Or-Eye-El*.

18. Vibrate *Around me flame the pentagrams. Above me shines the six-rayed star*.

19. Repeat the Qabalistic Cross Ritual.

Inner Working

At 3. visualize the lines of the pentagram being draw in blue fire, which emerges from your fingertips. The flame you get from burning methylated spirit is exactly the visualization you need here.

At 5. as you vibrate the name, imagine the sound rushing away from you eastward. (This is repeated at the other quarters.)

At 6. you should visualize the blue fire emerging from your fingertips as you move. This will then describe a quarter arc of a circle from east to south. The same visualization, carried through at the other quarters, will leave you surrounded by a closed circle marked by flaming pentagrams at each of the four quarters.

At 14. visualize a vast telesmatic figure of the archangel Raphael before you wearing shimmering robes of shot silk in yellow and mauve. Imagine cool breezes coming from this quarter.

At 15. visualize a vast telesmatic figure of the archangel Gabriel behind you, robed in blue offset by orange, holding a blue chalice and standing in a stream of swiftly-flowing water which pours into the room.

At 16. visualize a vast telesmatic figure of the archangel Michael robed in flame red flecked with emerald. He stands on scorched earth with small flickering flames at his feet and carries a steel sword. Try to feel the intense heat which emanates from this quarter.

At 17. visualize a vast telesmatic figure of the archangel Auriel, whose robes are a mixture of olive, citron, russet and black. He holds sheaves of corn in outstreched hands and stands within a very fertile landscape.

At 18. visualize (along with the ring of fire and pentagrams) a hexagram of interlaced triangles (like the Star of David) floating above your head. The *ascending* triangle (pointing upwards) is red in colour, the *descending* triangle is blue.

This completes the inner and outer workings of the pentagram ritual. I have gone into both in considerable detail because they seem to me to be relevant to the question of where you can go while projected and why certain places are barred to you.

The pentagram ritual is both an astral and a physical operation. The visualization activities would tend to create stresses in the Astral Light, acting as fiery barriers and fierce 'angelic' guardians against the intrusion of any astral entity. But conducting the ritual on the physical plane as well, links astral and physical structures. Thus the (physical) room in which you work is guarded too – not, of course, against physical intrusion, but quite possibly against etheric entry.

Any experienced astral plane projector will quickly confirm that the pentagram ritual *works;* at least in so far as establishing certain astral structures and cleansing the space within the circle. Whether it works at etheric levels is a little more speculative, but the odds are that it does. Empirical experience shows there are certain areas you cannot visit in a projected state and the suspicion arises that such places are in some way *protected* perhaps by structures similar to those set up in the pentagram ritual. It is a field ripe for experimental research and details of the pentagram ritual have been given in that spirit.

Do climatic or weather conditions influence projection?

There is some suggestion that it may be unwise to attempt projection during electrical storms or thundery weather when there is a high degree of positive ionization in the atmosphere. Otherwise, weather conditions do not appear to have any influence one way or another.

Do certain types of people project more easily than others?

While I have carried out no formal experimentation on this question, my experience has been that psychics, including mediums, tend to project easily and achieve deep-level hypnotic trances easily. Given that deep (hypnotic) trance subjects make good projectors, I have little doubt a three-way connection exists.

Outside of this, I have frequently noted that personality types prone to rational questioning frequently find projection difficult, if not impossible. The same holds true for rigid personality structures overlaying a lack of self-confidence. The best projectors seem to be those with a high degree of self-confidence, risk-takers unafraid of new experience, with intelligence and an ability to concentrate deeply and visualize clearly.

Could projection replace rocketry as humanity's most promising form of space travel?

I should very much like to believe that it could, but existing evidence is against it. Despite my references to projectors leaving the planet, almost all projective trips to other worlds within and beyond our solar system, have brought back descriptions of environments very much at odds with what we know of the structure of the universe.

Some early projectors, for example, described advanced civilizations on the Moon, Mars and Venus. Scientists have long considered this to be nonsense and space probes have since confirmed absolutely that the scientists were right.

When Carl Jung 'left the planet' in his near-death projection, he arrived at a rock floating in space. There are indeed rocks floating in space (they are called asteroids) but Jung went on to describe meeting human, or at least humanoid, entities living on it, without, apparently, benefit of water, food or air.

Clearly, visions of this sort are astral plane in nature and bear little or no relation to physical reality. Etheric projections beyond the planetary atmosphere may be possible, but I have yet to find convincing proof that they have been achieved. The one account which came closest was, curiously enough, that penned by the much discredited George Adamski, who claimed, in the Fifties, to have met a Venusian following a flying saucer landing.

Adamski later insisted that he had been taken on a flight in a saucer and circled the moon, giving humanity its first glimpse of the far side of the satellite. (The moon's axial rotation is so freakishly synchronized with its orbit that it always presents the same face to the earth.) His description of the hidden side was so naively bizarre – he spoke of roads and rivers and a thoroughly fantastic landscape – that even his followers found it difficult to take seriously.

Circumlunar probes subsequently showed the far side of the moon to be very similar to the near side: a cratered landscape. But these same probes also showed that when photographed from a certain height, lighting conditions on the far side of the moon create a peculiar optical illusion, so that the surface takes on an *appearance* strikingly similar to what Adamski described. Adamski was also the first to recount the peculiar 'firefly' effect noted later by several lunar astronauts.

If this is not all an extended coincidence, the question obviously arises as to where Adamski got his information. For many of his followers, there is no problem: he met a Venusian and was subsequently taken on a saucer flight. For those of us who find it difficult to accept Venusians whose body structure seems to have been formed by precisely the same evolutionary forces as shaped our own (or to accept Venusians at all, for that matter, given what we now know about the surface conditions of that horrid planet) the whole thing is much more difficult. Adamski certainly did seem to have discovered things about the moon and space flight which were only confirmed more than a decade later. If he did not find them out as a passenger on a Venusian spaceship then perhaps – just perhaps – he was an unusually talented projector.

Can animals project?
So far, available evidence seems to suggest humanity is the only animal with the ability to project an etheric body. But the Astral Plane is something else. Projectors have brought back many accounts of meeting with cats there and some insist their favourite dogs will follow them there.

Although it strains credulity, I have also to report astral plane sightings of cats which had previously died (on the physical at least.) When contact was made, these animals found it even easier to communicate with their human companions than they had done during their lifetime.

Is the Astral Plane the same thing as the Bardo Thodol of Tibetan Buddhism?

Yes. The most popular canon of Tibetan Buddhism in the West is the Tibetan Book of the Dead, which tends to give the impression that the Bardo Plane is a post-mortem state. Other Tibetan scriptures, however, make it quite clear that yoga disciplines will enable the adept to visit the Bardo while still very much alive. This, the ready equation of the Bardo with the dream state and descriptions brought back by Tibetan visitors to the Bardo all point to the fact that Bardo and Astral Planes are identical.

Are there mechanical aids to projection?

Apart from those already mentioned in the workbook, there are intriguing suggestions that one of the greatest structures of antiquity was, in fact, a machine to induce separation of the subtle bodies from the physical. This structure is the Great Pyramid of Cheops.

By any criterion, the Great Pyramid is an impressive building. It is situated on an artificially levelled mile-square plateau at Giza, about 10 miles west of Cairo, and set on a base that covers 13 acres. An estimated two and a half million blocks of limestone and granite went into its construction, some of them weighing as much as 70 tons – enough stone to build every cathedral, church and chapel raised in England since the time of Christ . . . and still have some left over!

There are more than enough mysteries associated with the Great Pyramid to keep archaeologists and associated scientists busy well into the next millennium. Its structure embodies the value *pi*, for example, while the pyramid is set, perhaps not coincidentally, on the line joining the Poles which passes through the greatest landmass. The precision of its building and orientation is little short of astonishing. In the dry air of Egypt, its peak generates substantial static electricity, giving rise to weird displays of ghostly lights in suitable weather conditions.

Conventional wisdom has it that the pyramid was originally built as a tomb for the Pharaoh Khufu (Cheops is the Greek version of his name) although no mummy or other indication of a burial has ever been found. There is, however, a sarcophagus of chocolate-coloured granite in a chamber set central in the pyramid and roughly one third the way up from base to apex. The sarcophagus – and the style of roof – has led to the chamber being known as the 'King's Chamber' with the assumption being that Khufu's body rested here until it and the treasure trove traditionally buried with a Pharoah was removed by grave-robbers some time in the distant past.

There are, however, problems with this theory, not least of which is the fact that Egyptian Pharaohs tended to worry themselves silly about grave-robbers since desecration of the mummy and certain statuary buried with it, put paid to hopes of survival in the afterlife. As a result of this paranoia, most Egyptian rulers elected to be buried in secret mausoleums rather than tombs so spectacularly public as to cause world-wide comment.

But if the pyramid was not intended as a tomb, the puzzle of its actual purpose remains. What benefit would persuade any culture to invest so much time and effort in a single construction? According to a number of writers, including Manly P. Hall, the answer lies in the Egyptian Mysteries.

Mystery religions were a feature of the ancient world in many countries. They were characterized by claims to secret knowledge revealed only after a candidate had passed through a series of tests in a process of initiation. In some mysteries, the initiatory process was largely symbolic, like the modern Masons. In others, the test involved drugs and dangerous, sometimes life-threatening, experiences. What secrets were eventually revealed is more a matter of speculation than certainty, but clues can usually be found in the culture which gave birth to the mystery. The Egyptian culture had, of course, one central obsession – survival of physical death.

This obsession led to the development of skills of mummification unparalleled anywhere on earth. Egyptian techniques of bandaging have yet to be matched, even today. The aristocracy invested much time and a goodly part of their fortunes in the construction of elaborate – and secret – tombs, which were as well-stocked as a submarine at the start of a long voyage. The mummy was accompanied by food, coin, weapons, clothing, ornaments, treasure and even guards and servants in the shape of specially commissioned statuary. Priests were paid substantial amounts to protect the tombs with magical charms and curses; and some appear to have earned their fees to judge from what happened to members of the expedition which unearthed the tomb of Pharaoh Tutankhamen.

Egyptian doctrine about the afterlife sounds peculiar to modern ears, for the Egyptians believed each of us is possessed of a number of souls. The *ka*, or double, was associated closely with the physical mummy. The *ba*, or bird soul, flew from the corpse at the moment of death, but liked to stick around so that a perch for it was usually provided in the tomb. The *ib*, or heart, went to the Judgement Halls of Osiris where it was weighed against a feather and condemned if found to be weighted down with sin.

Whatever about the Judgement Halls, students of projection will find much of interest in the remainder of Egyptian doctrine. The *ka*, for example, sounds suspiciously like the etheric body, while the *ib* might well be that more subtle vehicle destined to function on the Astral Plane.

But if the Egyptians knew about subtle bodies, it seems possible, perhaps even likely, that they also knew these bodies might be safely separated from the physical before death. And this is precisely what Hall and a number of other writers have suggested.

In all this, we are sidling sideways towards what is now popularly called pyramid power. Since a Czech inventor was granted a patent for a razor blade sharpener in the shape of a miniature pyramid, the eccentric and curious have gone to considerable experimental lengths to determine whether the geometric shape of a pyramid somehow attracts, generates or condenses a hitherto unknown form of energy. Certainly pyramids do *something*. Apart from renewing the edge on a razor blade, a pyramidical structure will preserve and dehydrate organic material correctly placed within it. Curiously, the correct placing of material in miniature pyramids actually corresponds to the placement of the King's Chamber in the real thing.

In an orgy of amateur experimentation which followed an upsurge of interest in pyramid power a few years ago, pyramidical tents were built as healing devices and aids to meditation, on the odd – and perhaps naive – assumption that a force which sharpens razors, slaughters bacteria and dehydrates meat has to be good for you.

One experimenter who might have voiced a warning had he been still alive was the English mystic and explorer, Paul Brunton. Before the Second World War, when the English still had some influence in Egypt, Brunton managed to get permission to spend a night in the Great Pyramid. In a moment of admirably courageous whimsy, he switched off his lamps and climbed into the granite sarcophagus in the King's Chamber. The chamber was filled with a curious inner light and Brunton plunged into a dramatic and frightening visionary experience.

It is, of course, entirely possible that the cause of Brunton's experience was auto-suggestion. He expected something odd to happen, so his unconscious obliged by creating a few showy hallucinations so he would not be disappointed. But that reference to the inner light is intriguing since it was mentioned by another visitor to the Great Pyramid, the notorious magician Aleister Crowley.

Crowley arrived in the pyramid during the honeymoon of his disastrous marriage to Rose Kelly and both witnessed the light phenomenon. Crowley, however, was quite familiar with it due to his experiments in ritual and projection. He recognized it at once as astral light.

Against this background, the theories proposed for the pyramid's purpose do not sound quite so outlandish. These theories hold that the pyramid, far from being a tomb, was actually a Hall of Initiation. Candidates seeking entry into the mysteries were taken into its gloomy interior and, after various trials, laid out like Brunton in the granite sarcophagus. There, pyramidic energies caused the automatic separation of the subtle bodies and the Initiate projected either as an etheric ghost or an excited voyager into the luminous environments of the Astral Plane. Either way, he would return to his body convinced that life after death was a literal reality.

Can women project more easily than men?
No. There seems to be no sexual differentiation in the ability.

Does diet make a difference to projection abilities?
As noted elsewhere in this workbook, claims have been made that it does, but my own experience has failed to confirm this. Whatever about your general diet, however, projections attempted immediately following a heavy meal are less likely to succeed than at other times. The same mechanism has led to the sound advice that you should always eat something – even if only a biscuit with a cup of tea – immediately after you return from a projection session, since it will help 'earth' you again.

Is projection a relatively new talent?

Far from it. As we have seen in the answer to an earlier question, there are suggestions the Ancient Egyptians knew all about it. But even they were latecomers to the art.

The world's oldest religion is Shamanism, a system of belief that reaches back, quite literally, into the mists of prehistory. Shamanism is with us still, in primitive communities worldwide – and is enjoying an unexpected revival at the time of writing in Britain, where it actually has its own magazine.

Central to Shamanism is the figure of the Shaman, a sort of priest magician whose training is almost exclusively aimed at inducing astral plane projection. The ability is achieved through rigorous training, sometimes involving the use of herbal drugs, and trance states brought on by dance and drumming.

Is there any connection between projection and sex?

Yes. Spontaneous temporary projection at the point of orgasm is not exactly an every day (or every night) occurrence, but it is not particularly uncommon either, although those involved are often too distracted to recognize it for what it is. Because of this, sexual systems of projection have been developed, although the use of sex as an aid to projection is more usual in the Orient than the West.

Can anything I do on the Astral Plane influence events on the physical?

As much as 90 per cent of magical practice as taught in Western esoteric schools is based on the assumption that it can. Much of this arises out of Qabalistic doctrines. Central to modern Qabalah is the glyph known as the Tree of Life, which incorporates 10 circles, symbolizing spheres of function in the nature of reality, and the various paths which join them, indicating, among other things, the complex interrelationships of the Tree.

At the risk of over-simplifying, the bottom Sephira (sphere) of the Tree – called Malkuth by Qabalists – signifies the physical aspect of reality, or, more practically, the world in which we live.

Directly above Malkuth is the sphere of Yesod, associated with lunar function and symbolizing the self-same astral plane which has been the subject of so much discussion in the present workbook. The English title of Yesod is *foundation*, chosen because the word is indicative of the essential nature of the sphere. For to Qabalists, Yesod, the sphere of imagination and Astral Light, is the literal foundation on which physical reality rests.

This stands on its head the viewpoint which has dominated the present work – the idea that the Astral Plane is so malleable that the simple presence of certain physical structures (such as mountains) can actually influence its landscape. But while the most apparent and obvious influence flows from the physical to the astral, a far more profound influence actually manifests in the other direction.

A moment's thought will produce some justification at least for the notion. Granted that the Astral Plane is intimately linked with human imagination, we can clearly see that great symphonies, novels and works of graphic art all begin to develop on the astral long before they make an appearance in physical reality. Thus, in a very real sense, the astral structure forms a *foundation* for the physical.

But the process does not begin and end with works of art. Buildings have astral beginnings as architects draw up their plans. Inventions appear on the Astral Plane before the first physical prototype is constructed. A little more abstractly, emotional relationships have inward beginnings, as have many political ideas and social movements. This is all little more than the old observation that the thought is father to the deed. But magical practice takes the whole thing substantially further.

A glance at the description of the pentagram ritual given in an earlier answer shows that it has two aspects – the inner and the outer workings. All ceremonial magic follows this pattern and it is the hidden nature of the inner working which enables much magical technique to remain secret even when its physical aspect has become public knowledge.

Analysis of even the simplest magical operation reveals, in almost every case, the same twofold aspect. One of the most primitive examples of magic involves the use of a *moppet* which stands in place of the human being at whom the spell is aimed. Countless horror stories have been written round this theme, generally illustrated by the Voodoo doll into which a multitude of pins have been inserted. Sympathetic magic ensures that when a needle is driven into the thigh of the moppet, pain is felt in the corresponding part of the victim's anatomy. Yet common sense – and even a little careful experimentation – soon indicate that nothing of the sort occurs, otherwise every little girl's doll named after a relative or friend would wreak havoc when it was accidentally broken.

Yet moppet magic *does* work in the hands of an experienced practitioner; and can be used to cure as well as harm. But it is not the moppet which does the trick. The actual magic is in the mind of the individual who uses it. The doll is, in point of fact, no more than the focus of visualization – an astral operation. The real simulacrum of patient or victim is created on the Astral Plane, with the doll serving as a physical link. What is then done to the astral model eventually manifests in the physical body of the target via the individual's own (often quite unconscious) linkages with the Astral Plane.

This is a spectacular, if limited, example, yet empirical experience indicates that whatever structure is built on astral levels has, if stabilized, a tendency to manifest eventually on the physical.

Are there planes beyond the astral?

Yes. Just as the Astral Plane can be reached by moving from the etheric in a new direction, so can other, even more subtle planes, be reached by moving *upwards* out of the astral. . .

Oriental yoga (and by association systems like Theosophy) classifies these planes as:

Upper Astral
Lower Mental
Mental

Higher Mental
Lower Spiritual
Spiritual
Higher Spiritual

With the addition of the astral we have already been examining, this creates a mystical seven as the number of inner planes, although the number probably has more significance in the minds of those who enjoy classification than it does in reality.

The labels commonly given to these levels are not particularly helpful, although they do purport to tell us something about the nature of the plane described. Thus, while the Astral Plane is associated with the imagination, the mental planes are held to be linked in some way with the more abstract modes of mentation, while the spiritual planes are associated with our most elevated and subtle sensitivities.

But if this gives little indication of what the remaining planes are actually like, some projectors may find they have the capabilities of experiencing some or all of these subtle levels directly. Not everyone can do so, and the further 'up' the levels a projector tries to go, the more difficult entry into ensuing planes becomes.

The effort to find one's limitations is, however, worthwhile, since the subtle planes have features of as much interest as the astral, but far less well-explored. Some present intriguing experiences indeed. One projector with whom I worked found herself functioning without sight on a plane in which she could nonetheless sense entities she recognized as angels. They were powerful, unidirectional and surprisingly lacking in warmth.

Index